Criticism and Faith

John Knox

~~~~~~~~~~~~

Criticism and Faith

ABINGDON-COKESBURY PRESS

New York • Nashville

CRITICISM AND FAITH

Library of Congress Catalog Card Number: 52-8843

Quotations from the New Testament unless otherwise designated are from the *Revised Standard Version*. Copyright 1946 by the International Council of Religious Education.

SET UP, PRINTED, AND BOUND BY THE PARTHENON PRESS, AT NASHVILLE, TENNESSEE, UNITED STATES OF AMERICA

To
FRANK LEIGHTON DAY
of
RANDOLPH-MACON COLLEGE

GRATEFULLY AND LOYALLY

Foreword

BECAUSE of the personal character of much in this book, there is little need of a personal preface. We shall be concerned with a very important, and for many of us a very poignant, problem: What bearing does the historical method of studying the Bible have upon Christian faith? This is a perennial problem of Christian youth, especially youth from a conservative or orthodox background, and, I am convinced, is the continuing or often recurring problem of many older Christians who have long since given formal assent to the method. On one hand we find it difficult to deny the truth and relevance of the method; on the other we find it intolerable to depend on its results at any vital point of faith.

Some stimulation to the preparation of this book was undoubtedly provided by my experience of serving during the past five years on the editorial staff of a biblical commentary, *The Interpreter's Bible*, which is seeking to utilize the contributions of both historical scholars and expository preachers as interpreters of the Bible. It has been my privilege not only to supervise some of the historical exegesis which has entered into this work and to write a very small part of it, but also to attempt the expository treatment of some of the gospel material (a treatment from which I have borrowed somewhat in Chapter VI of this book). This experience confirmed my belief not only that the preacher has something distinctive to contribute to the interpretation of the Bible, but also that this "something" must be historically true if it is true at all. But if preaching must keep close to history to be true, biblical historical scholarship must keep close to preaching to be important—or indeed, at least so far as the New Testament is concerned, to be even true, for the New Testament is itself a record of preaching.

This reference to New Testament scholarship as distinguished from biblical scholarship as a whole reminds me to warn the reader that in the following pages I may often have passed from the one to the other without explicitly making this distinction and without indicating clearly the point of transition. In much of this book we are looking at biblical criticism in general; but often attention is being focused on the New Testament particularly, and sometimes, even more narrowly, on the gospels. Occasionally in the same paragraph all three of these perspectives will be involved. To explain the shift of focus in each case would seem both unnecessary and awkward, but the consequence of omitting to do so may sometimes be a lack of precision and consistency, for which I must ask the reader's indulgence.

Four of the chapters of this book were, in substance, presented as the Jackson Lectures at Southern Methodist University, and the other two as the McFadin Lectures at Texas Christian University. The honor bestowed and the many courtesies extended by each of these institutions are gratefully acknowledged.

Although the last chapter and some parts of earlier chapters deal especially with preaching, the problem of this book is more than a problem of how the functions of the biblical critic and the biblical preacher should be differentiated and defined. The problem is a broader one: that of determining how dependent Christian faith is upon biblical historical scholarship. Can scholarship seriously impair faith? Can scholarship significantly aid it? The answer to be given to the first of these questions is "No" and to the second, "Yes."

The fact that after a century or more of historical biblical scholarship these questions can still be raised points among other things to a failure which a teacher of the Bible can perhaps with greatest appropriateness acknowledge. This is our failure so to grasp and use the historical method as to make clear that it not only does not threaten us or place in jeopardy any important Christian value, but also offers us possession of great spiritual riches; that to understand the Bible historically is to find deeper meanings and larger values in it than can otherwise be gained; in a word, that the historical method is also the most creative method.

JOHN KNOX

9

Contents

CHAPTER I

Historical Criticism:
Welcomed or Forced on Us?

IT was little more than a half-century ago that modern biblical criticism, already widely received abroad, first seriously challenged us in America; and remarkable even for these rapidly changing times is the extent to which in the brief interval its method and presuppositions have become assimilated within the American church. One hardly needs to add that this result was not achieved easily or without conflict. Many of us will remember how poignant the issue was—how strange, impious, and ominous seemed the suggestion, when it was first made, that the Bible was in most respects a human book to which the methods of historical research developed in the study of other ancient literature were fully applicable. We will remember the spiritual agony we suffered when we were forced to recognize such facts about the Bible as low moral standards in parts of it, historical inconsistencies, scientific misconceptions, and the like—haunting facts, which we tried to deny but could not forget, and which

13

seemed to threaten our deepest and most precious securities. But many will also remember how they emerged from this struggle with the conviction, held more strongly and clearly than would have been possible before, that the Bible, although far from being a magically infallible, a verbally inspired and inerrant book, nevertheless not only is incomparably the most important book in our Western cultural tradition, but is in a unique sense *the* book, absolutely indispensable and supremely significant for the church and for all mankind, and very bread for the soul.

This history of challenge gradually accepted and of opposition gradually overcome is fully taken for granted in this discussion; there is no need to resume old controversies or to fight over old battlefields. Most of the readers of these pages will long since have approved in principle the historical method of studying the Bible and will have no interest in formal defense or even formal definition. It may be appropriate and useful, however, to attempt at this juncture some appraisal of the significance of the method and some inventory of its results: To what extent has the historical method been really accepted by the church, that is, with a full understanding of its implications and consequences? Has the currency of the method meant loss to us as well as gain, or (if one looks at it so) gain as well as loss? What effect has it had, or should it have, on the way the meaning and authority of the Bible are conceived? What bearing does it have on Christian faith? What is its effect upon preaching? With such broad and essentially religious and theological questions we shall be concerned in these discussions.

I

The question with which we begin may seem quite gratuitous and irrelevant: To what extent has the historical method been really accepted among us? Someone will say: "Surely we do not need to discuss that. It is true that a generation ago there was significant fundamentalist opposition to biblical criticism, but the back of that opposition was broken in the twenties of this century. Historical method has come, and it has come to stay. Let us go on from there." Such remarks, however, although they may represent a natural first response to the proposed question, fall short of being critical and realistic observations. Let us look at the facts—facts first about others and then about ourselves.

There is at the outset the obvious fact that only within Western non-Roman Christianity has the historical method of Bible study enjoyed any significant degree of approval and acceptation. Eastern Orthodoxy has, to say the least, not encouraged the method. Although the Eastern church has produced its critical historians and has left them relatively free from censorship and restriction, nevertheless little critical work has been applied to the Bible, and in any case the influence of critical historiography on the masses of the people has been negligible. Roman Catholicism has virtually outlawed and

15

banished the method. To be sure, its use is permitted within certain prescribed limits; but to set limits to the applicability of historical method, except the limits of history itself, is in principle and effect to repudiate it. One of the most discouraging elements in the present tragic separation between Protestantism and Roman Catholicism is the virtual fundamentalism of the Roman Church. This can be said with full and grateful recognition of the growing interest in the Bible in that church and of the important contributions to our knowledge which some of its great biblical scholars have made. If the Modernist movement, whatever its faults, had been allowed to run its course and to have its true effect, the prospects of a united church would undoubtedly be brighter. But as it happened, that movement was destroyed—the von Hügels, the Tyrrells, the Loisys were discredited, if not excommunicated—and the Roman Church was officially committed to the necessarily divisive view that historical questions can be answered by dogmatic pronouncement. When we say, then, that the back of fundamentalism has been broken and that the right of the historian has been vindicated, and even his duty established, to deal with all historical questions, no matter how intimately they may seem to bear upon important concerns of Christian faith, and to deal with these questions with complete freedom, that is purely and simply on the basis of the relevant data—when we make such an assertion, we are ignoring the situation in the larger part of Christendom.

16

But how true is the assertion even as applied to the Anglican and Protestant minorities? We are hearing much nowadays of the important and growing section of Protestantism which is confessedly fundamentalistic. But to the hundreds of thousands who belong to explicitly fundamentalist bodies must be added the millions who belong to professedly nonfundamentalist bodies but are themselves all but entirely ignorant of the meaning of the historical method of studying the Bible and in any case quite unprepared to accept it. These are not for the most part self-conscious and militant fundamentalists: they are simply naïve. One of the most distressing features of church life is the theological gulf between the seminaries and graduate schools on the one hand and great multitudes of lay people on the other. Why is it that so many theologically trained leaders have theologically illiterate congregations? Why is it that, eating bread and meat ourselves, we have often continued to feed our people only milk?

To answer this question adequately would involve consideration of the whole educational technique of the church. For such a task I am certainly not competent. I venture to suggest, however, that the principal reason for our failure to get across to our congregations the necessity and the value of historical method in the study of the Bible lies in the fact—with which much in these chapters will be concerned—that many who have accepted historical method in principle do not fully believe in it and have not fully assimilated it. Is it not often

17

true of us, of biblical critics as well as of others, that we have accepted the method, not because we have gladly seen in it great creative possibilities, a means of enriching the life of the church, but because we have been forced to it? Growing scientific and historical intelligence or the need for a solution of certain immediate and painful problems arising in the course of our efforts to interpret the Bible to our generation has thrust the method upon us. In so far as this is true, our acceptance of it has tended to be reluctant and partial, not wholehearted, unreserved, and complete. Historical criticism has appeared to many as an enemy with which they manifestly have to come to terms. Its help subsequently can be, it is rather grudgingly conceded, of some limited value; but it is not a friend of whose important aid they are eager to take advantage. The responsibility for such a situation cannot be simply or easily assessed. The causes are complicated and difficult to define. But can we deny the fact that, for whatever reason, we are generally speaking in this double mind about biblical criticism? We have accepted it, yes; but as churchmen, whether we are critics or preachers or laymen, we are likely to have our suspicions and inhibitions.

II

When one seeks the reason for this uncertainty, if not distrust, one is bound to find it partly in mere impatience with what appears to be the religious irrelevance of much biblical research. Biblical study often seems to exhaust itself in an examination of various linguistic and historical details. No one can make the slightest excursion into the scholarly study of the Bible without discovering that it is literally crammed with the most fascinating literary and historical problems. Problems of the text of documents, of their integrity, date, authorship, place of writing, historical occasion, their diction and style, the time and circumstances of their canonization—such problems are innumerable and for anyone with even a trace of the antiquary's or the explorer's instincts irresistibly attractive. No detective-story writer would want better puzzles, with fewer clues, than the Old Testament or the New Testament scholar can find merely by looking about him on any side.

Such study not only is fascinating but is often of the largest importance, and we must be on guard against a premature dismissal of it. One cannot always see how relevant an apparently irrelevant fact may prove to be. One cannot approach an understanding of the Bible except through linguistic and historical study (that of others if not also one's own), and the approach is not always direct and plain. But when all of this is said, it must still be recognized that the biblical study which exhausts itself in mere linguistic and historical exercises and does not ultimately contribute to the understanding of the meaning and message of the Bible or of the nature and history of the ancient church can hardly hope to be regarded as important by the church—or even by the critics themselves if they are also churchmen.

Biblical scholarship stands in an ambiguous position. On the one hand it is a purely academic discipline, a branch of archaeology, of paleography, of ancient literature, language, and history. As such its affinities are with the other branches of these general disciplines. But it is not these affinities which account for the greater part of the importance which biblical study has. These affinities are not to be denied, and the linguistic and historical effort applied to the Bible must be as skillful and as rigorous as that applied to any other literature; but biblical study is really important because it is a branch of theology—because of the light it throws upon the life and thought of the Christian community in its earliest and most formative epoch and upon the great event in which it was born, Jesus of Nazareth, the Son of God. Study of the Bible which does not, directly or indirectly, add to our understanding of this event and of its meaning and consequences in the church cannot be really significant. Some biblical study has unquestionably been of this arid and irrelevant sort.

For many, however, the major reason for distrust of the critic has not been this aridness and irrelevance, whether real or fancied. He may have been neglected or disregarded partly on that account, but he has not been merely neglected and disregarded. He has been to a degree disliked and suspected, and the reason for this antipathy and suspicion has not been a recognition of his irrelevance. Indeed exactly the reverse is true: he has seemed too dangerously relevant. It has seemed to many that

20

issues crucial for our faith are involved in the answers he finds it possible or necessary to give to the questions he studies. To cite one example: When I am invited to address a group of ministers on the present state of gospel criticism, I often detect in some of my audience a certain wistful eagerness for at least a part of the assurance they once felt about the gospels. They have no hope that either I or anyone else can fully restore that assurance—all that the critics have done cannot be undone. But they hope that I can at least say that scholarly judgment on the whole supports the more conservative as against the more radical critics, or can assure them that in my opinion something will be left in the gospels despite all that the critics have done or may yet do, and that therefore they will still have some kind of gospel to preach. It is one of the major purposes of this book to show that this apprehension is utterly groundless—that biblical historical criticism not only has no stranglehold on Christian faith, but does not have it in its power to destroy one jot or one tittle of the gospel. The ground of this assurance will appear in the next two chapters; just now it may be well to mention several grounds frequently alleged or assumed which must be rejected as specious or inadequate.

III

One may note first that the immunity of faith from any peril from criticism does not rest on any arbitrary restricting of the historian's field. His method when once invoked cannot be limited. It cannot be permitted to deal with some historical questions and enjoined from dealing with others. Many Christians, recognizing this, have steadfastly refused to open any of the historical statements of the Bible to free historical inquiry; there is more logic in this, the fundamentalist, position than in that of other Christians who have been willing to let the historian look at some of the biblical facts but not at all of them. They have been willing to accept the historian's help in getting out of such difficulties as those presented by the crude anthropomorphisms in some of the primitive parts of the Old Testament or by the minor contradictions among the gospels, but they rather wish he would voluntarily refrain from asking the same kind of question and applying the same kind of method in seeking the answer about the life of Jesus or the traditional authorship of the Fourth Gospel. But such a limitation cannot be imposed either by the historian upon himself or by others on him. Until the boundaries of history itself are reached, we simply cannot say to the historian, "Thus far only can you go!" "Sacred history" is as certainly subject to the historian's examination as any other kind of history.

Nor does the conviction that historical criticism holds no real threat to faith involve the claim that faith has some peculiar faculty of its own for securing historical knowledge—knowledge which takes precedence over the findings of the historian. A contemporary scholar for whom I have great respect writes (in a context which has to do with questions of historical fact): "I hold with subjective certitude many beliefs . . . which objectively must be accounted uncertain." [1] I doubt that such a statement can bear scrutiny. What right have we to feel certainty—indeed how can we—about what is recognized to be uncertain? We may in certain situations of "forced option" act decisively and irrevocably without being "objectively" certain, but in such an event we lack "subjective certitude" also; we take a conscious risk. It must also be acknowledged that in the realm of existence, of concrete experience, one knows much, and knows it with absolute certainty, which no amount of "evidence" would enable another (who does not have the same experience) to know. But to say that in this case the certainty is "subjective" and not "objective" is hardly accurate; at any rate the person who feels the certainty would not be satisfied with such a statement. He will not be ready to say, "I hold with subjective certitude what objectively must be accounted uncertain."

[1] Walter Lowrie, *The Short Story of Jesus* (New York: Charles Scribner's Sons, 1943), p. 6. I have hesitated to make so brief a quotation knowing how often a writer's meaning can be misrepresented by a single sentence taken out of a paragraph or section. I do not believe, however, that a reader of pp. 3-8 of Dr. Lowrie's beautiful book will feel that any injustice has been done. In fact it seems to me that those pages well illustrate the confusion as regards the relation of historical criticism to faith with which this book as a whole is concerned. One is left with the impression—or half-impression—that strict historical method in dealing with historical questions in the gospels is assumed to be incompatible with either the poet's appreciation or the believer's insight and devotion. This assumption—so widely if tacitly held—is in my judgment not only untrue but baneful.

23

He will feel that the objective facts fully support his inner conviction. Otherwise "subjective certitude" is not only without justification; it is psychologically impossible. If this is true of our knowledge in general, it is even more true of our knowledge of history: faith is among other things a way of *understanding* history, but not a way of learning the facts of history. What one knows of these facts, one knows from one's own experience or from the testimony of others—there is no other way.

Finally it must be urged that the claim of faith's freedom from any threat from historical criticism does not rest on any view of Christianity as aloof from or independent of history. The distinctive, central item of Christian faith is that God supremely revealed himself in Jesus Christ. This was the essential meaning of the earliest Christian confession, "Jesus is Lord," and has been the essential meaning of every Christian confession since. Christian faith is not belief in natural revelation, although of course that kind of revelation is not excluded. Nor is it belief in the divine authority of some inner voice or in the divine truth of some esoteric wisdom. The Christian does not look about him or within him for the source of his light; rather he looks to an ancient event, although the light from that event is conveyed to him within the life of a continuing historical community and although it illuminates his present life in every part, outer and inner. He looks to an ancient event—here we have the fact which separates

24

Christianity from every variety of gnosticism, ancient or modern.

> The Church's one foundation
> Is Jesus Christ her Lord.

Christianity, then, is by definition a religion for which history is of supreme concern; a historical event is indeed the very source and center of it.

To say this is to affirm the importance of the historian and the pertinence of his method in the study of it. But to say this is not to make the historian the sole and final arbiter of faith. In so far as we have regarded him as such, fearing that to acknowledge his right to deal with our Christian historical sources was tantamount to delivering the Christian faith into his hands—to that extent we have not properly understood (and this has often been true also of the historian himself) the real nature of the event which brought the Christian community into being and is in a sense perpetuated in its continuing life. The next two chapters will be concerned with the meaning of that statement.

The Security of Faith

THE major consequence of the historical study of the Bible over the last half-century might be formulated in some such way as this: Scholars of the Old Testament and of the New have placed beyond any doubt that the books of the Bible sprang out of the experience of the religious community, Hebrew-Jewish and Christian; that the Bible did not create the church but was in fact an expression—the supreme literary expression—of the church's life. For this reason it should be studied and can be understood only in the light of the character, interests, experiences, needs, and circumstances of the historical community whose life it reflects.

To any student of general literature this will sound like an utter commonplace. Imagine anyone's trying to study Plato except against the background of the political, social, and intellectual situation in Athens in the fourth century B.C., or Milton without seeking an intimate knowledge of Puritan England. Or, to cite a more adequate analogy, imagine someone's trying to understand

26

English literature as a whole without constant reference to the life and thought of the English people over the centuries of the nation's history. But the persistence of a magical view of the Bible's origin both delayed the discovery that this general principle applies to the Bible no less than to other literature and also made the discovery, when it came, more startling and revolutionary.

The intimate involvement of the Bible with the life of the historical community could be indefinitely elaborated and illustrated. The historical books of the Old Testament are efforts to describe and interpret the origins and development of the Hebrew nation. The psalms are the hymns of the temple after the Exile. The prophets speak about events occurring or threatening to occur within the nation or in its relations with other peoples. The epistles of the New Testament are concerned with problems of faith and practice which have arisen in the primitive Christian communities. Even the gospels can be understood only when it is recognized that they reflect the interests and are addressed to the felt needs of the Gentile churches in the late first and early second centuries.

Not only are all the books of the Bible addressed to the religious community and concerned with its experiences and its needs; they also, as has been said, spring out of its life. The writers of the Old Testament histories and prophecies and of the New Testament gospels and epistles are all members of the Hebrew-Jewish or of the Christian community, and they all speak simply and only as such. This is true not only of the less eminent

27

writers who come fairly near to representing the ideas and actual practices of the rank and file of the devout, but also of the great creative writers, such as Amos, Isaiah, Paul, and John. These latter, for all their genius, speak as members of the community and are inconceivable apart from it. These great books are concerned with the contemplation and interpretation of realities within the community's experience and survived just because the community as a whole recognized in them a setting forth of its own true and authentic life. What these great writers possessed of special insight had been mediated to them through the life of the community in which they were nourished. This is particularly true—or rather true in a special sense—of the writers of the gospels. Indeed it is being increasingly clearly recognized that these gospels are not so much the work of personal authors as they are compilations of a corporate tradition. The gospels are in a special sense community books. They put into what has proved to be final form the materials of mixed reminiscence and interpretation of Jesus which had accumulated and circulated in the churches immediately following his career.

The first consequence then of the application of historical method to the Bible has been the realization that the Bible is a record and reflection of the experience of a more or less continuous and coherent historical community, and that more particularly the New Testament (with which we shall be especially concerned in these chapters) is the literature created by and expressing the life of the Christian church during the first several decades of its history.

1

Now one cannot read this literature without recognizing that the community whose life it reflects stands in the immediate glow of a great event. Something has happened which has brought the community into being, has determined its basic character, and now rules its life. This event was remembered as centering in the life, death, and resurrection of Jesus and was interpreted by the community as nothing less than God's decisive act for the salvation of mankind. Through it God had created a new order of being, a new community, in which the hostilities, the conflicts, and the frustrations of our earthly existence are finally overcome.

This new order was the order of the Spirit and was only partially realizable within history. But it was partially realizable there, and the church was this partial realization, this "first fruits," this "earnest" of our inheritance. The church was the culmination of the event, and in it the event was both mirrored and perpetuated. For the event was in its essence the coming of the Spirit; and the church was in its essence the people of the Spirit. Indeed one may say that the event with which the New Testament is concerned can be defined essentially and exactly as that particular occurrence or cluster of occurrences through which the Spirit was given and the church

29

was brought into being, and that it can be essentially and exactly defined in no other way.

It will be clear that if this statement is true, the event has a status both of absolutely indisputable historicity and of supreme religious and theological significance. As for historicity there can be no possible question that the church had a historical beginning and that this beginning was the culmination of an actual historical happening or development. Something happened to bring the new community into being, and if that "something," whatever it was, is the event we are discussing, we know that it took place. The very existence of the church contains the fact of its occurrence. Moreover, as we have seen, the New Testament was a by-product of the same historical development that produced the community. It brings us a living picture, so to speak, of the church in the very process of being created. And if the church-being-created *is* the event-being-enacted, then it brings us a living picture of the event also. How the picture can be most truly interpreted and how the event can be most fully recovered are matters with which we shall be occupied later. At the moment we are concerned only with the fact that the subject of the picture is by definition the event and that the historicity of the latter is therefore indisputable. There can be no doubt that we possess the New Testament and that it brings us the beginnings of the church and thus the fact of the event.

But the *significance* of the event thus defined is equally surely established. For to say that in and through it the Spirit came and the new community was created is to attribute to it all the divine meaning which Christian theology and devotion have ever found in it. It is to affirm nothing less than that at a particular moment in our history God acted to make himself known to men concretely and effectively in a new and supremely authentic way as Love and Truth, and that in the new community which he thus created he continues to dwell with men, making available forgiveness, healing, reconciliation, and a new righteousness—in a word it is to identify with the event the whole meaning of Christ in the New Testament. Is there any more exalted way of conceiving of the significance of the event? Thus when we define the event as that historical occurrence or cluster of occurrences which culminated in the coming of the Spirit and the creation of the church, we affirm everything that Christian faith could possibly ask as to its meaning, and at the same time we place its historicity beyond any possible question.

"But," it is objected, "the definition is inadequate. We must know more than this about the event or else we have no basis for faith in its significance—or in the significance of the church. The church rests on the event, not the event on the church." This last statement is true, and much will be made of it later in our discussion (especially in Chapter IV): the church *does* rest on the event. But whatever *knowledge* we can have of the event must be derived from our own experience in the church, from the testimony of others in the church,

31

or from the New Testament, which is itself a record of the experience of the church at the time when the event was actually occurring or had just occurred. It is obvious, for example, that we do not have some prior or independent knowledge of the life of Jesus which enables us to test how accurately he was remembered. We have only the early church's memories of him. Similarly, it is not because we have some prior and independent knowledge of the Resurrection or of Pentecost (that is, as definite historical incidents) that we accept the fact of the presence of Christ or the Spirit in the early church; rather the belief in the Resurrection or in Pentecost is possible only because Christ (or the Spirit) was so manifestly present in the life of the community. And only on that account, it may be added, does such a belief have any significance for us. There could be no meaning or substance in anyone's belief that there was once a man named Jesus, or that the Spirit came or Christ arose at this time or that, or under these circumstances or those, if one had not first become aware through participation in the experience of the community of the creative power of the memory of the man Christ Jesus, of the reality of the Spirit, and of the newness of life in Christ. While it is true, then, that the significance of the church rests upon the significance of the event, it is also true that we are able to *attribute* significance to the event only because we find it first in the church. We can know the historical event only as it is remembered and interpreted and perpetuated in the historical community.

32

But this is after all what a historical event is; that is, an event is not something hypothetical and unrecoverable which lies before or back of the experience of the persons to whom and among whom it occurred; a historical event is this "something" as it was received and responded to, as it was remembered and interpreted, as it became creative in history. When the event Jesus Christ is described in these terms, there can be no doubt that it occurred. The very existence of the church and the very existence of the New Testament bear irrefutable witness.

We have been concerned so far with the formal definition of the event: What is it precisely and essentially? Its concrete meaning and both the richness and the limits of our actual knowledge of it will come more fully into view as this discussion proceeds.

II

We are now in position to ask about the possible threat of historical method to faith. This question will be discussed in the next chapter also, and the reader is requested to withhold judgment as to both the meaning and the truth of the position being presented until that chapter also has been read.[1] But we may now make a beginning by asking three questions about the event of which we have been speaking, considering particularly

[1] Perhaps it may also be appropriate to refer to a small book of mine, On the Meaning of Christ (New York: Charles Scribner's Sons, 1947), in which an attempt is made to explicate the meaning of "event" as that term is used in this discussion also.

33

just how dependent we are upon the biblical historian for our answer in each case. The three questions are: Did the event occur? What was its significance? and, What was it as an objective historical occurrence?

As to the first of these questions—Did the event occur?—two remarks may be made. On the one hand the virtual irrelevance of historical criticism at this crucial point needs to be reaffirmed. The assured positive answer we find ourselves giving to this question of bare historicity does not depend at all upon the biblical historian's having first satisfied himself of its truth. Our knowledge that the event occurred is not a conclusion based on the critical examination of documentary evidence. That knowledge is *given*—that is, to be a Christian is to find oneself possessing it. For to be a Christian means to belong to a historical community; and just as we do not need the historian to tell us that the community is historical or that we belong to it, so we do not need him to tell us that it had a historical beginning. Something happened to bring the community into being, and that "something" not only is enshrined in the New Testament (gospels and epistles), but is carried in its memory and witnessed to by its continuing life. We do not need the historian to tell us that it occurred, and it is only less inconceivable that the historian should ever inform us that it did not occur than that we should believe him if he should. In other words the biblical historian cannot "hurt" us or decisively help us at this point. We are not speaking, it must be remembered,

34

of the actual content of the event, but of the formal fact of its occurrence. That fact is implicit and undeniable.

On the other hand the historian by making us aware of the intimate connection between church and event enables us to see this implicit fact in a way in which we could not have done without his help, and although it would be too much to say that the Christian believer is made more sure of the event than he would have been otherwise, he is undoubtedly put in position to see more clearly why he is sure and how impregnable his essential position really is.

Virtually the same two comments seem called for on the bearing of historical criticism upon the second of our questions, What was the significance of the event? On the one hand it may be said again that at the crucial point we are not dependent on the historian. The Christian answer, as we have seen, may be stated in some such way as this: The event was an act of God on our behalf. In what happened God visited and redeemed us. He did this by bringing into being a new community in which he was known in a new way as grace and truth and in which the possibility of repentance, forgiveness, and new life was made available. We certainly do not need the historian to tell us this is true. If we find it true, we do so because we are Christians—that is, we have been made members of the community and participants in its meaning—and not because we are either historically informed or historically ignorant. But on the other hand it needs to be said that although the historian

35

could not conceivably destroy this meaning, he can make us more aware of the range and depth of it by opening up to our understanding the variety of forms under which it was received and interpreted by those who first knew it. This service of criticism will be discussed later.

This brings us to our third question, What was the event as an objective historical occurrence? The phrasing of the question is hardly satisfactory because of the false suggestion it carries that an event can ever be defined entirely objectively. Perhaps a better form of the query would be: What were the circumstances and incidents which together with the responses made to them and the meanings found in them constituted the event? Here it must be recognized not only that the biblical historian has the right to speak but also that at most points he alone has that right. In so far as we give anything like a definite or detailed answer to this question, either we are being historians ourselves or we are following other historians—and the only question is how good as historians we or our guides are. Christian faith and the experience of the Spirit within the Christian community can never give us the answer to this kind of question. If we think they do, we are deceiving ourselves. One accepts by faith, if one accepts at all, the fact that God was "in Christ reconciling the world to himself"; but one who supposes that faith provides any answer at all to the question of where Jesus was born, or who wrote Ephesians, or what was the original meaning of the Lord's Supper, or when Jesus was first believed in as

36

the Christ, is mistaken. These are purely historical questions, and only the competent historian can give a competent answer. One is no more in position to give true answers to such questions simply in virtue of being a Christian than one can know the date of the Declaration of Independence or the name of its author simply by being a patriotic American.

And yet even here there is a certain small but essential minimum of historical truth of which the Christian believer is so sure that, although the right and duty of the historian to look into it are gladly granted, it would not be true to say that the believer is ever in any doubt about the outcome of that scrutiny or that his own knowledge is in any real sense dependent upon it. I have in mind here what is ordinarily known as the "historicity of Jesus." But this phrase is abstract and somewhat misleading. More exactly I am referring, not to any fact *about* Jesus, not even to his "historicity," but to the person himself as, living and dying, he is remembered in the church. It is impossible for the Christian to entertain any real doubt of the existence of this person, for the memory of him is an essential element of the Christian life itself. Now the fact that the man Jesus can be known only as he is remembered—that we have no prior or independent, no "objective," knowledge of him—was noted earlier in this chapter. But we have also seen that it is *Jesus as he was remembered and interpreted* who is alone important for the Christian community. It is *this* Jesus with whom both faith and history are concerned. The perception of this fact invests the whole New Testament picture with a kind of immediate and unquestionable historical value: the event of Jesus Christ was precisely that totality of fact and meaning—of fact responded to, remembered, and interpreted—which is indubitably set forth in the New Testament (gospels and epistles) and is thus itself indubitable. We are not, therefore, under any religious or theological "pressure" to separate nicely between fact and meaning and to say exactly where one leaves off and the other begins; as a matter of fact the two are fused indissolubly. But although it is not necessary for the Christian to distinguish or identify the element of fact, it is inevitable that he shall affirm its existence: something *happened*. In other words to recognize that the man Jesus in the church is a person *remembered* is on the one hand to recognize the impossibility of dividing neatly between what he was and what he was remembered as being, as well as the comparative irrelevance of trying to do so; but on the other hand this recognition involves also the inescapable implication of historicity. One cannot remember what one acknowledges may never have existed.

This historicity, it must be noted again, is not exempt from the historian's scrutiny; and if it were discredited by that scrutiny, it would have to stand discredited. Actually, however, the Christian believer is not in the position of being dependent upon the historian at this point—the reason being, not that he denies the right of the historian to deal with the question of Jesus' historicity, but that he knows so surely what his answer will be.

This statement may seem at first to involve a contradiction. How, it may be asked, can we open any historical question freely to the historian's scrutiny, acknowledging his prerogative without reservation or limitation, without at the same time being dependent on him for the truth? Without meaning to suggest any analogy beyond the point under discussion may I offer an illustration?

Imagine a historian approaching you with the proposal that with your approval and assistance he write a biography of a deceased friend whom you knew intimately and loved well for many years. You have complete confidence in the historian and gladly give your approval, turning over to him all the data you have. He goes his way and for several months or years is engaged on his research and writing. Now under these circumstances you do not have the slightest doubt of the appropriateness, the applicability, and the reliability of historical method and of the historian's right and duty to look at every phase of your friend's life; but at the same time you are not at certain points in the slightest degree doubtful of what his findings will be. In particular you are sure of the historicity of your friend: the man you remember existed, and in his personal character, especially in his relations with you, he was essentially and substantially the man you remember. The historian may enlighten you at many points; he may prove that you have been mistaken about many of the facts of your friend's

39

life, perhaps surprisingly many. He may even prove that in the years since your friend died your picture of him has to a degree undergone a change of focus and that you "see" him now somewhat differently from the way you used to see him (whether more or less truly is another question). All of this he may do, and you would need to acknowledge your obligation to him. But on the matter of historicity you do not need his help. You are already sure. You remember your friend.

In a way not too different the church bears in its heart the memory of Jesus and would find inconceivable that the historian's method should ever discredit that memory. To be a Christian is not simply to believe something or even to experience something, but also to remember something. Indeed this memory, running back continuously to the very beginning, becomes the major piece of evidence for the historian's inevitable conclusion. The existence of the church is the principal historical evidence for the historicity of Jesus; he who stands within the church does not need even this evidence. Others may doubt that Jesus lived; it is impossible that he should.

An additional reference must be made to what is in many ways the supremely precious fact for the Christian—the fact of the Resurrection. It is clear that the primitive community's knowledge of the risen Jesus is an indisputable historical fact. But the believer is sure, not merely of this knowledge on the part of the first believers, but of the reality of the Resurrection itself. This reality the believer knows, knows beyond peradventure, knows without any fear of what the historical scholar has discovered or may discover. Any historical proof that the Resurrection did not take place is simply inconceivable, for the basis of our assurance of it is not documentary but experiential—the actual presence within the life of the community of one who makes himself known as the one who is also remembered. It is this reality (in the New Testament often called also the Spirit) which makes the church the church, constitutes its center and the very principle of its being. Thus to speak of the Resurrection is to speak not only of the organic unity of the event, with its historical elements and its divine meaning, but also of its continuity with and in the life of the community. And, conversely, to recognize, as every Christian finds himself doing, this unity and continuity—the very one remembered is still known—is to affirm the fact of the Resurrection, and to affirm it with complete and unqualified assurance, without fear that any historical evidence can possibly discredit it.

III

We see, then, that the blame for a good part of the church's distrust of the biblical critic must be laid upon a false idea, entertained not infrequently by the critic himself, of the importance of the questions of fact with which he is often concerned. That the historical event which we call "Jesus Christ" occurred and that through it God acted to bring into being a new people, a new order of salvation—these essential matters are beyond the reach of any historical criticism. That the event had at its center the human career of Jesus, a career of such kind that God could make such supreme use of it, and that it culminated in the Resurrection—here too we are standing on our own unassailable ground. Some of these matters, to be sure, fall legitimately within the field of the historian and are properly subject to his scrutiny; but it is inconceivable that he should either discredit them or give them for the Christian any needed or decisive support. Apart from this essential structure of Christian faith, it is true, the historian not only is free (he is always free to deal with all historical questions although we are not always entirely dependent upon his answers), but has sole jurisdiction and competence. On these matters we must rely on the historian alone. Only by the application of historical method can any assured knowledge be obtained. But why should we wish it otherwise? There is no reason for anxiety. Just as nothing in Christian life and experience can provide this knowledge, so no essential of Christian faith depends on it.

In order to see more clearly that this is true it may be well for us to note a few points where it is most severely tested—to consider, that is, some questions with which the biblical historical critic has concerned himself and with which he must concern himself if we are to have valid knowledge, but which we have often regarded as being so important to Christian faith that we could not unreservedly commit them to his care.

42

CHAPTER III

The Meaning of Christ

WE have been concerned almost since the beginning of this discussion with trying to understand the grounds for a certain chariness, if not hostility, in our attitude toward the historical method in Bible study. We have accepted it—there seems to be nothing else to do—but not without reservations and not with our whole hearts. As citizens of the twentieth century we have been forced to come to terms with it, and we have reluctantly acknowledged that in certain ways it can help us; but we have not gladly embraced it. The alliance most of us (critics and others) have made with critical historical method has had strictly limited objectives and has not been free from mistrust. Some of the reasons for that mistrust we have been considering in the preceding chapter. It manifests itself in at least two ways: first in an inclination on our part to require more in the way of evidence for the establishment of a nontraditional position in the field of biblical study than would be required in other fields; and second in a virtual refusal to accept the results of disinterested historical study if supposed theological and religious interests seem to be placed in jeopardy.

The center of this theological and religious interest for the Christian is of course Christ, and our apprehension and resistance increase the nearer the biblical critic seems to be coming to that center. The reason we tend to require anywhere within the field of biblical literature and history a stronger case for the abandonment of a traditional position than would easily suffice outside that field is that the Bible is pre-eminently the literature which directly or indirectly is concerned with Christ. For this same reason we are likely to feel more apprehension about historical criticism of the New Testament than of the Old and of the gospels than of the epistles. And when criticism ventures to question a biblical statement about Jesus himself—his ideas, his personality, or his life— our first reaction is almost certain to be hostile and resolutely defensive. Other questions have struck at the ramparts; these threaten the citadel iself. The major purpose of the foregoing chapter was to show that this attitude is not justified; no such crucial issue hangs upon the biblical historian's work as we have sometimes feared. That same purpose will engage us in the present chapter, where we shall be concerned primarily with the problem created for many by the application of the historical method to the life and teaching of Jesus.

44

I

At the outset it must be gratefully acknowledged that any willingness to make distinctions within the Bible as regards value or as regards degree and kind of certainty represents an advance upon the older fundamentalism. There was a time, I suspect, when some of the readers of this book, along with its author, were disposed to say: "Unless all of the Bible is equally true, and true in the same sense, we cannot know that any of it is true at all." No wonder we resisted so stubbornly the plain indications of error and inadequacy on the part of its writers! Undoubtedly, as we have seen, an important element in the true solution of this problem for the believer lies in the acknowledgment that some statements of the Bible can make an absolute claim to truth which other statements cannot make.

But it is important that we realize the true character of this distinction. It is not a distinction between statements in the Old Testament and statements in the New, or between statements about the life and words of Jesus on the one hand and statements about the life and words of Paul and others on the other hand, or indeed between any two sets of historical statements one of which is regarded for any reason as being more important than the other. We cannot, it must be said again, adopt piecemeal or part way the historical method of studying and assaying the historical materials in the Bible, applying it faithfully to that part of the historical material

45

which we consider of only subordinate importance, but renouncing it or at any rate neglecting it when the material is concerned with some vital fact. All of these ways of distinguishing between statements of the Bible are irrelevant and arbitrary; the distinction which alone is appropriate and justifiable is the distinction between those statements, important or not, which are purely historical, that is, are concerned simply and only with past incidents and developments, and those statements which are confirmed in the continuing life and experience of the Christian community.

We saw in the last chapter that there are some historical statements which are also statements—or at least necessary implications or presuppositions—of Christian faith. But these, although they are the only crucially important historical statements, are few in number. All of them have to do with Christ, and we are reminded of the Johannine text of Jesus' words: "You search the scriptures, because you think that in them you have eternal life; and it is they that bear witness to me; yet you refuse to come to me that you may have life." (John 5:39-40.) Scriptures for this writer meant of course what we call the Old Testament, but the statement that Christ is the real subject of scripture as well as the implication that he is more than scripture stands true for the Bible as a whole and in particular for the gospels. Christ, borne witness to by the gospels, is not confined within them; nor is he borne witness to by them alone. He is the living reality at the center of the church's life. No historical study of the Bible can place that reality in jeopardy. The recognition of this fact can free both faith and study—faith from needless and distracting anxieties and historical study from the obstacles which the fears of the faithful have often placed in its proper path.

In order to probe more fully the meaning of this fact let us discuss three affirmations: first, our knowledge of Christ does not depend upon what can be known about the life of Jesus; second, our knowledge of the authentic words of Christ does not depend upon what can be established as Jesus' words; and third, the truth about the meaning of Christ does not depend upon what was present in the self-consciousness of Jesus.

II

First, then, our knowledge of Christ is not dependent upon what can be reliably known about the historical life of Jesus.

As we saw in the preceding chapter, when we go beyond the church's memory of Jesus himself, we move out of the area where its own essential life gives any answer to the historical question and into the field where we must depend upon the historian if we are to have any assured knowledge at all. When was Jesus born and where? What is known of his ancestry? What schooling did he have? What can we know about his home life? Did great miracles mark his birth and indeed his whole career? What was his occupation or trade? When and how did he receive his vocation to a religious ministry?

47

What precisely was that vocation? How long did his public ministry last? What took place in it, and in what order did the incidents occur? Who were his friends, and who were his enemies? When and where was he put to death, and on what grounds? Did Resurrection appearances occur? If so, to whom and when and where?

To such questions as these can it be seriously argued that the essential life of the church provides any answer? Are we not entirely dependent upon the New Testament documents? But to say that we must rely upon these documents is to say that we must rely upon them as examined and tested and interpreted by the same methods appropriate in the study of documents generally when used as sources for historical facts. And to say this is in turn to say that any answers we give to these purely historical questions must be given tentatively, subject to criticism and modification. Moreover since in many cases the evidence of the gospels is not clear and decisive, different answers to the same question are bound to be proposed and defended by historical scholars of equal competence and integrity.

Such uncertainty about matters connected with Jesus himself is likely to be disturbing, and to many it seems quite intolerable. Religious faith requires certainty. One must know what one believes. Religious faith is a complete and final commitment; it is not a tentative acceptance. But the solution of this difficulty does not involve the tour de force of believing "by faith" what is or may become susceptible of proof or disproof on historical grounds. The solution lies rather in the recognition that Christian faith, however full, unreserved, and authentic, involves not the slightest measure of commitment on such facts about Jesus' life as we are now discussing.

The Christian faith in Christ, as we saw in the preceding chapter, is faith in the significance of the event in which God acted for us men and our salvation; both the fact of this event and its significance rest on other than merely documentary grounds and are believed in by the Christian without reservation or condition. Jesus is remembered as the central element in that event, and therefore his existence cannot be doubted by the Christian. But no mere incident or circumstance of Jesus' career belongs to this memory, possesses this indubitability, or shares in this importance. One can, as one should, examine any alleged incident or circumstance with the same freedom one feels in examining a similar datum in the story of any other historical personage. The answer one gives to the question of whether Jesus was born in Bethlehem or Nazareth is as far from having essential religious significance as is the position one takes on such questions as the date of Homer or the identity of Shakespeare. The more positive implications of this affirmation will be clearer as we consider the other closely related statements proposed for consideration in this chapter.

III

Our second affirmation was that our knowledge of the authentic words of Christ is not limited to what can be established as Jesus' words. It is probably true to say that at no point has the application of historical method been more resented and resisted than at the point of Jesus' teachings. The "words of the Lord" have from the beginning had peculiar and supreme authority in the church. To raise a question as to the authenticity of the words ascribed to Jesus in the gospels has seemed to many to threaten this authority and therefore the whole order and security of the church.

If this question is raised, however—and how can we avoid raising it?—only the historian is qualified to answer it; for it is one of the "purely historical" questions which fall entirely within his province. Either Jesus said the words attributed to him on any particular occasion, or he did not, and we deceive ourselves if we suppose that our religious faith can tell us which alternative is true.

No one who studies the gospels with his eyes half open can miss the grounds for doubting some of the utterances attributed to Jesus. We shall have occasion in another connection to consider the anti-Semitic utterances (see pages 75-78). There are utterances of other kinds which on the one hand do not suit well the character and times of Jesus, and on the other do suit well the situation and interests of the later church, and are therefore on that account at least partly suspect. A comparison of the gospels discloses divergencies in the way Jesus' teachings are reported which simply cannot be accommodated within the uncritical, naïve view that Jesus said just what the gospels attribute to him. Did Jesus say the Beatitudes in the form in which we have them in Matthew or in their Lukan form? (And to recognize that he may have said them in either form is to recognize that he probably said them in yet a third form which neither evangelist has exactly reported.) Did Jesus respond to the rich ruler in the way he does in Mark and Luke or in the quite different way described in Matthew?

These are examples, chosen at random, of variations minor in extent and significance as compared with others in the gospels, especially if the Fourth Gospel is taken into account. Given any understanding at all of the process by which Jesus' words were communicated and handed down and of the practical purposes they served in the developing church, these variations will seem natural and inevitable; but to recognize this means to acknowledge that a certain measure of doubt must attach to every particular saying. We may be sure that Jesus said a certain kind of thing, but never quite sure that he said just this thing or that. But doubt in a matter of such importance is likely to cause even the critical student of the New Testament, if he is a Christian believer, some pain and anxiety, while to many it will seem inadmissible and insufferable.

But this misgiving and anxiety are quite inappropriate and unnecessary. The words which are of greatest and deepest concern to us as Christians are not the words of Jesus but the words of Christ, and the authenticity of these words is not established and cannot be impugned by criticism higher or lower. The words of Christ are

51

the words which truly and at firsthand set forth the meaning of the event, which is Christ, and therefore the meaning of the church's true life. Those words attributed to Jesus in the gospels which set this meaning forth are authentic words; those which do not set it forth truly or are not concerned with it are *not* words of Christ.

The words of Christ in this most important sense are the words of God—or, better, formulations of the Word of God. This Word of God is not a word at all but a deed. The Word of God is what God did in and through the event of which Jesus was the center. Since this event was the eschatological event, since this act of God was the final saving act, Jesus is the Christ; and we can speak of what God did "through Christ" and can call the event itself or the act itself by his name. Thus Paul writes, "In Christ God was reconciling the world to himself." The event culminated in a new community through which this reconciliation is mediated and conveyed and in which therefore the event itself is continued and perpetuated, not simply as something remembered, but as a living, present, and creative reality. This living, present, and creative reality—sometimes called the Spirit in the New Testament, sometimes Christ—is continuous with Jesus of Nazareth but is not to be simply identified with him. The words of the Spirit are as certainly the words of Christ as are the words of Jesus. To deny this is to deny the reality and significance of the Resurrection. If Christ still lives, we have no right to limit his authentic utterances to words spoken by human lips in Galilee or Judea.

It is this fact that Christ in the Spirit continued to speak which lies back of and under the Fourth Gospel's presentation of the words of Christ. The writer of that gospel is seeking to convey the meaning of the total event, Jesus Christ, as that meaning has made itself known to him, a member of the new community of the Spirit; and the greatness of his gospel consists in the fact that he has done this so superbly. To be sure, he is casting his material in a dramatic biographical form and therefore must place the words of the Spirit on the lips of Jesus, but hints of the truth keep breaking through, as, for example, in 14:25: "These things I have spoken to you, while I am still with you. But . . . the Holy Spirit, whom the Father will send in my name, he will teach you all things, and bring to your remembrance all that I have said to you"; or even more clearly in 16:12-15: "I have yet many things to say to you, but you cannot bear them now. When the Spirit of truth comes, he will guide you into all the truth; . . . he will take what is mine and declare it to you. All that the Father has is mine; therefore I said that he will take what is mine and declare it to you." The truth that breaks through such utterances as these is that many sayings attributed to Christ in this gospel were recognized by its author as being not remembered words of Jesus of Nazareth at all, but words of the Spirit—that is, they embody truths disclosed within the experience of the new community where the living Christ is known. This does not make them any less the words of Christ but more.

These words of Christ no historical criticism can invalidate. Such criticism may demonstrate that they were not first spoken during the historical career of Jesus, but it cannot place them outside the limits of the event which included that career but also much more, and with which alone the New Testament is really concerned.

Here we see a characteristic error of both the fundamentalist and the modernist. Both identify the creative, revealing, redemptive event simply with the career of Jesus. For the fundamentalist this means a refusal to apply historical method to the study of the career, since to make the career subject to free inquiry is, as he sees it, to place in jeopardy the whole significance of Christ. The modernist on the other hand, does not hesitate to apply historical method; but because he shares the basic presupposition of the fundamentalist that the whole meaning of Christ is located in the historical career of Jesus, he is likely to end with a purely naturalistic view of the revelation in Christ, thus seeming to justify the fundamentalist's apprehensions. The fundamentalist, assuming that there cannot be words of Christ which are not words of Jesus, ends by refusing to deal intelligently with the gospel records of Jesus' words. The modernist, making precisely the same assumption, ends by reducing to pitiable meagerness, uncertainty, and futility the words of Christ. But both are wrong, and wrong for the same reason, even though the results seem so different: they both identify the saving event with the his-

54

torical career. In the one case this means the obscuring and distorting of the career; in the other the virtual negation of the event. The realization that the true words of Christ are words of Christ, whether spoken within the limits of the historical career or not, should free us from both errors.

IV

The third affirmation proposed for consideration was that the truth about the meaning of Christ does not depend upon what can be discovered as to the way in which Jesus himself thought of the meaning of his career.

We are familiar with the fact that in Jesus' own time the coming of the kingdom of God was conceived of variously: sometimes as coming directly as the consequence of an unmediated act of God; sometimes through the agency of the Messiah, usually a son of David; sometimes through the mediation of the Son of Man, a heavenly person to whom God would in the fullness of time commit the functions of judgment and redemption. How did Jesus think of the kingdom's coming? And how did he think of his own relation to it? Was it coming simply by God's direct action, and was he the prophet of its advent, calling men to repentance so as to be prepared for it? Or did he expect the appearance of the Messiah or the Son of Man? If so, which? And again, how did he think of himself as related to this appearance? Was he the herald of it? Or did he regard himself

55

as actually being the Messiah or the Son of Man? Did Jesus, knowing that he was the Messiah–Son of Man and foreseeing his suffering and death, bring together into one conception the glorious Son of Man of Daniel and Enoch and the humble suffering Servant of Isaiah, or did this synthesis emerge only after the Resurrection? Did Jesus intend and deliberately establish the church?

All such questions, concerned with the self-consciousness or what has been called the "intention" of Jesus, are of paramount historical interest and importance. No student of Jesus' life or of the history of the beginnings of Christianity can evade them, or will wish to. But we are mistaken if we suppose that any vital concern of faith is involved in the way we answer them. The meaning of Christ is not limited to the terms in which Jesus conceived that meaning. The relation of Christ to the church is not affected by the way in which Jesus thought of that relation. In actual fact the real substance of all the hopes of Israel, in whatever formal terms this hope was expressed, was (as the Christian sees it) fulfilled in Christ; but this does not mean that Jesus must have appropriated and applied to himself each or any of these terms or even that he thought of himself as fulfilling the hope in some more general sense. The point here is not that he did not do so, but rather that it does not greatly matter whether he did or not. The meaning of Christ is not restricted to what was present in the self-consciousness of Jesus.

Just as we have tended to identify the whole redemptive event with the person of Jesus of Nazareth and to localize, so to speak, God's saving action within the limits of a historical career, so we have been inclined to identify the whole meaning of the event with ideas in Jesus' mind. But while the meaning of the event is not subject simply and only to the biblical historical critic's scrutiny and judgment, the ideas of Jesus about eschatology and Christology do fall within his province. The historian may not be able to reach a clear and certain conviction of what these ideas were, but until he does, the rest of us must be in doubt. There is no other source of light. We are not justified in assuming that the experience of the church provides us with any answer to the historical question at this point. But, on the other hand, uncertainty here does not affect even slightly our assurance of the meaning of Christ.

Indeed nothing given by faith or important to faith is endangered even slightly by any answer we may give to any controversial historical question or by any uncertainty we may feel with respect to it.

One cannot make such an assertion without suggesting two questions, which we must now examine. The first is: Why, then, do we consider or trouble with these questions of historical fact if the answers we give to them have no essential or even important connection with faith? The second is: What importance or authority does the New Testament have, since the norm of Christian truth seems to consist so largely in the life of the church itself? To these two questions, considered in reverse order, the two following chapters will be devoted.

CHAPTER IV

The Authority of the New Testament

THROUGH the last two chapters we have considered the reasons for confidence that we have nothing to fear from the historical student of the New Testament as regards any matter vital to faith—that this faith rests upon what is given within the life of the church and that no historical research can possibly take it away. But, as we have noted, the acknowledgment of this fact suggests a question, not only as to the positive value of biblical historical research (the matter to be discussed in the following chapter), but also as to the importance and authority of the New Testament itself. "Does this not mean," it may be asked, "that the source of authority in the church is the church itself? Does it not involve complete surrender of the evangelical position and virtual acceptance of that of Rome?" Since I should say that this is not true, some further clarification of the position set forth in the preceding chapters is obviously called for.

I

We may begin by recalling that in all that has been said about the source of light and truth within Christianity two factors, rather than one, have been named: the event and the community. These two factors exist in the closest possible interrelation. All historical events occur in a social context, among or within human groups, for people and to people; and this social context belongs to the very being of the event as such. An event without the social response to it is not an event; it does not belong to history at all. Now the event of which Jesus is the center and which we call by his name is no exception here. It happened to persons, among them and within them; and their response is intimately and inseparably a part of it. The church is more than the social consequence of the event; more even than the social milieu in which it occurred; it belongs to the very existence of the event itself.

It is on this account that we have so much difficulty in saying precisely when the church began. For when are we to say that the event began? In one sense we cannot say at all, for like all events it is so inextricably involved in the interminable skein of history that it cannot be said to have beginning or end, except of course the beginning and end of history itself. Defined in another way, the event may be thought of as beginning with the beginning of Israel's history or with the emergence of Israel's consciousness of being Yahweh's covenant people.

59

In a stricter sense—and this is the sense in which the term is ordinarily used in the present discussion—the event began with the career of Jesus.

We are speaking of the event, but precisely this same ambiguity or indefiniteness must characterize any answer we give to the question about the church's beginning. It is not false to see in ancient Israel the beginning (and not the mere background) of the church and for certain purposes and in certain contexts to identify the two. It is certainly true to say that when Jesus called his first disciples, the church had begun to be. The community began with the event and moreover came ever more fully into existence as the event gradually unfolded. The church did not clearly appear until the event had reached its earthly culmination in the Resurrection and the coming of the Spirit, and it will not be fully itself till the event is fulfilled in the kingdom of God.

At every stage, then, event and community are indissolubly involved with each other. Whatever qualities or meanings are ascribed as essential to the event must be ascribed also to the community; whatever values are found as essential within the community must be attributed also to the event. To stand under the shadow of the event is to stand within the community; to stand within the community is to stand under the shadow of the event.

And yet, as this last sentence will have suggested, for all the closeness of this relationship it is clear that the event has a certain precedence. One stands "within the community" but "under the shadow of the event." It is certainly nearer the truth to say that the church exists because the event occurred than to say that the event occurred because the church exists (although of course we can *know* of the event only through the church). The church is in very truth the bearer of the revelation in Christ, and that revelation is a continuing act of God; but the act originally occurred at a given time and place; and that original moment, just because it was the great creative moment, is the normative and authoritative moment. Event and community thus stand toward each other not in correlation only but in tension.

This was true at the very beginning. The event as it transpired was constantly embodying meanings which the community could not comprehend and making demands which the community could not fulfill. "Depart from me, for I am a sinful man," said Peter to Jesus; and when Jesus and his disciples were "on the road, going up to Jerusalem, . . . Jesus was walking ahead of them; and they were amazed, and those who followed were afraid." Something was happening which far transcended both their understanding and their capacities for moral response. At the cross they "stood at a distance and saw these things"; and what they "saw" was not something merely within or among them but something far above and beyond them. And when with the Resurrection the church came more clearly into being, its members were able to describe what had happened only as the advent of the Spirit; something belonging not to this world at all,

61

but to another world and another age, had miraculously come to them. So closely associated was the community with the event that they were able to designate it with Christ's own name: to be in the church was to be "in Christ." But to be "in Christ" was to be within a community which was also "under Christ." The event had precedence and authority. So it has always been and must always be. When the church loses contact with the event, it has lost contact with the source and norm of its own true life; it has ceased to be the church.

To say that the event has this normative value is to say that the earliest period of the church's life has an importance which no subsequent period can have. The first age of the church reflects and embodies the event in its initial character and impact in a way no later age can hope to do. To be in touch with the most authentic life of the primitive church is to be in touch with the original event—the most direct touch we can have. It is correct to say that we can know Christ only through the church; at this point the Catholic idea is true. But when we say "only through the church," we do not mean only through the contemporary church or even the church through the centuries. For it is given us to have contact directly with the primitive church, the church within whose experience the event occurred in a sense in which it cannot occur within ours, and whose experience has therefore a normative significance, unique in degree and kind. This direct contact with the primitive community is made possible through the Bible.

62

The authority for the Christian, then, is the authority of the event, for our knowledge of which in its initial impact we are dependent upon the experience of the primitive community which it called into being. But we are put in direct touch with this experience only in and through the documents which that community produced. Here we have the clue to the understanding of the paradoxical character of the Bible's relation to the community. On the one hand it is less than the church because it grew out of the life of the church and has meaning only within the context which that life still provides, but on the other hand it is greater than the church because it brings us the only record we have of the event through which the community was brought into being and therefore provides the only means for its constant renewal. This is the ground of the Bible's authority. And it is a ground undeniable, empirically verified, which no literary or historical criticism can shake; indeed, as we shall see in the following chapter, the principal value of historical criticism is that it establishes this ground more firmly.

The Catholic, then, is right in recognizing that the "substance" of Christianity is the church; that the revelation of God in Christ took place and continues to take place only there; that the very word "Christ," whatever additional meanings it may have in different contexts, always presupposes the community. But he is wrong in so far as he ignores the distinctive and distinguishable significance of the event with and in which the church

63

came into being. That event took place within the community and cannot be known except as it is found there; but when it is denied its own objective, independent character, when it is completely absorbed within or identified with the life of the church, the church is deprived of a norm for her own life which is absolutely indispensable. This Protestantism saw, and in turning to the Bible for this norm Protestantism was following right lines. But in so far as it found this norm in the Bible itself rather than in the event to which the Bible bears witness, it did violence to the nature of the church. For the norm of the church's life is not verbal—whether the words are those of ecclesiastical councils and bishops or those of the gospels and epistles—but is the revelation of God in Christ, which is a historical event. This event, like any event, is concrete and complex, incapable of being reduced to words or of being exhaustively described. But the Bible brings, out of the period when it occurred, an "eyewitness" account of it; and this firsthand account, although subject to criticism like any other account of a historical event, must be allowed to declare its own independent testimony.

When the church completely "absorbs" the Bible into its continuing life—that is, overshadows it, dominates it, denies to it objective and intrinsic value—when the church thus neglects or rejects the Bible, it separates itself from the historical event which brought it into being and must always be the historical source and norm of its reality as the church. But, on the other hand, when it sets up the Bible as being itself this source and norm, it separates itself from the event equally effectively, although in a different way. In both cases the event is ignored or obscured. The topic will be discussed in the next chapter, but it may be well to point out here that the chief value of the historical study of the Bible is that it helps us avoid both of these errors: to keep clear the integrity and independence of the event, distinguishing it (in spite of intimate interrelationships) both from the church on the one hand and from the Bible on the other.

II

It is the importance of the event as distinguished from the continuing church which explains and justifies a New Testament canon; that is, the very existence of the New Testament as a closed collection bears witness to this importance. The New Testament in its present form was not finally adopted until the end of the fourth century, but by A.D. 200 the conception of a closed canon was well established in the church. The four gospels, the Acts, and the letters of Paul belonged to all the lists of accepted books; the standing of other books varied somewhat among the various churches and church leaders. Alexandria's canon was more inclusive than Rome's, and Rome's than Antioch's; but the idea that a certain limited number of Christian documents had canonical authority prevailed everywhere.

65

But on what basis was canonicity determined? Why were the twenty-seven books belonging to our canon eventually approved and others rejected? Was it that these were intrinsically superior to all others—the deepest or wisest, the most enlightening or the most edifying, the most inspired or the most inspiring books which the church had produced up to that time? It would be hard to show that such books as Titus or II Peter qualify under such a definition. Besides if innate superiority was the criterion, why should the canon have been closed? That is, why should there ever have been a canon in the true and definitive, the exclusive, sense of the term? Superior books might yet appear; indeed superior books did appear. Who would deny the superiority of much, for example, in Augustine to much in the New Testament if the basis of judgment is simply intrinsic, whether literary excellence, inspired thought, or theological and religious genius? No; the justification of a closed canon must be, not the superiority of its member books to other documents produced by the religious community, but the *uniqueness* of these books. Canonical books are in theory not better than all others but different from all others.

But in what does this difference consist? The ancient church found the answer in apostolicity. Only what had been written by an apostle could be considered canonical. Canonicity and apostolicity became almost synonymous terms, apostolic authorship conferring automatically canonical quality or status. The argument moved both ways: II Peter, since it was presumably written by an apostle, must be accorded canonical status; Hebrews, because it obviously deserved canonical status, must have been written by an apostle.

There is some difference of opinion among students of the canon as to just when apostolic authorship was settled on as the decisive criterion of canonicity. Harnack held that it was in the time of the Montanist controversy at the very end of the second century and the beginning of the third, when the church had special need to appeal to an authoritative tradition from the past against a contemporary prophetic movement which acknowledged no authority except "the Spirit." But much can be said for a date a half-century earlier, when the New Testament as an authoritative collection was first taking form. The immediate impetus for the formation of this collection was apparently provided by the heretic Marcion, who, having rejected the scriptures of much of the church (what came later to be known as the Old Testament), set up a new scripture for his followers—a scripture in two parts, the Gospel and the Apostle. The Gospel was a single document which cannot be identified with certainty, but which closely resembled our Gospel of Luke; the Apostle was the ten letters of Paul which had earlier been collected. When, around A.D. 160 or 170, what proved to be the orthodox or catholic church responded to this challenge with a New Testament canon of its own, that canon took this same bipartite form. But now both Gospel and Apostle are enlarged: the Gospel is fourfold, and the Apostle in addition to letters of Paul (thirteen of them) contains the "Acts of All the Apostles" (so the Muratorian list of about A.D. 200 calls the book of Acts) and as many letters of other apostles as could be found. The criterion for membership in the Apostle was of course always and by definition apostolic authorship, and Irenaeus as early as A.D. 180 or thereabouts was at pains to point out that each of the four gospels was written either by an apostle or under an apostle's direction. The struggle with Montanism may have accented the note of apostolicity, but that note was present and important from the very beginning.

Now this stress upon apostolic authorship was in considerable measure inept and false. Apostles were not different from other men in gifts or endowment, nor did they receive some peculiar kind of inspiration. The apostles were men like ourselves, and there is no reason to suppose that all of them were persons of any extraordinary merit or were capable of any extraordinary spiritual discernment. Besides it is simply impossible to attribute all of the writings of the New Testament to apostles. Only on the basis of dogmatic presuppositions can one convince oneself or others that Paul wrote Hebrews, or John the disciple the Fourth Gospel.

But despite this measure of ineptness the church's appeal to apostolic authorship as the criterion of canonicity was based on a true insight. This insight is that the norm in Christianity is a historical event. The essential mark of canonicity is therefore proximity to that event. Apostolicity was an inexact but available and manageable way of defining this proximity.

This nearness to the event implies something as to intrinsic character. No document, however early, which was "remote" from the event in the sense of being palpably false to the meaning of Christ as remembered and still known in the church could have won recognition as the work of an apostle and therefore as a part of the canon, whether the falseness manifested itself in doctrinal or ethical ways. No document, for example, which defended either Docetism or libertinism could have been regarded as apostolic, no matter what its claims and no matter how plausible otherwise these claims might be. But so far as formal definition went, the decisive test was nearness to the event in a simpler, a more purely chronological sense: something supremely important, something unprecedented and in certain essential respects unduplicable, occurred in Palestine in the first century; documents produced in the first glow of that event, representing immediate responses to it and reflections of it, have a value and importance which make them as unique among books as the event had been unique among events. Every document which gained access to the New Testament can hardly be said to have this fresh and original character, to stand thus near the event; but the

69

collection as a whole can be thus characterized, and the ancient church in settling upon apostolic authorship as the essential criterion undoubtedly had this character in mind.

It was the church's insistence upon the crucial and normative significance of the event (as against all forms of gnosticism) which assured the formation of the canon. Just as the event originally called forth the several primitive documents, so the recognition of the importance of the event led inevitably to the collection and canonization of the documents. And just as to exalt the event meant to create the New Testament, so to exalt the New Testament, in the only way in which it can be truly and appropriately exalted, means, and has always meant, to rediscover the event which called first the church and then the New Testament into being, and remains the norm of both.

CHAPTER V

Creative Interpretation

W E must now return to a question which was raised explicitly only at the end of Chapter III, but which is certain to have been often in our minds in the course of this discussion. The question may be put in some such way as this: "You have been concerned to show that the questions of historical fact with which the historical critic deals are not issues vital to faith, even going so far as to say that nothing given by faith or important to faith is endangered even slightly by the answer he may give to any such question. If that is true, of what value is the historian's work? Is it not reduced to irrelevance and futility? You say the biblical historian cannot hurt us—but can he help us? Let it be granted that the critical movement of the last century and a half has not irreparably damaged our faith and does not have it in its power to do so—still has it contributed anything? If we are not worse off, are we any better off because the critic's work has been done and is being done?" This is obviously a crucial question in this discussion.

71

Theology can be classified in various ways. For our present purpose it is useful to distinguish between what may be called apologetic and confessional theology: the apologetic is concerned with formulating the Christian faith in such ways as to make it as intelligible and persuasive as possible to those who do not yet share it, the confessional, with explicating the faith so as to enrich its meaning and enhance its value for Christians themselves. Now the question proposed in the preceding paragraph is clearly asked not from the apologist's but from the confessor's point of view: Has biblical historical criticism enriched or is it capable of enriching the church's own life? And with that question we shall be dealing for the most part in this chapter.

It is important to observe, however, that the distinction between apologetic and confessional theology, while useful in discussion as representing a real difference in orientation and emphasis, must not be pressed too far. It is often argued that the original "apologists" for Christianity (in the second and third centuries) were writing quite as much to confirm the church in the truth of its faith as to persuade those outside. This double character of effective apologetic is inevitable in the nature of the case, and besides there is always external occasion for it. It is inevitable because the apologist cannot deal effectively with doubts and objections unless he understands them, and he cannot understand them without to some extent sharing them. One cannot so write or speak as to convince others unless one is also in some degree trying to convince oneself. But apologetic must have this double character or direction for another reason: Christians are never simply or only Christians; they belong to their generation and are affected by all the social, political, intellectual, and other forces which move through it. Any successful dealing with a skeptic's doubt is likely also to have the effect of confirming a Christian's faith. For these reasons, although we shall be concerned in the present chapter primarily with the contributions of biblical criticism to the church's own life, we need make no attempt to separate neatly between this contribution and the services of the method in apologetic, or entirely to exclude the latter.

Indeed so important have been the services which biblical criticism has rendered in the apologetic field that we must begin this part of our discussion with some reference to them. The fact and nature of these services have been touched on more than once and are not being discussed at greater length only because they are so generally recognized and acknowledged.

I

The apologetic value of the historical method is an aspect of what was hailed near the beginning of this book as its major achievement: namely, its having enabled us to see that the Bible is the literary deposit of the religious life and thought of the historical community, Hebrew-Jewish-Christian, in its most creative and formative period—the literature thrown off, for all its priceless worth, as a kind of by-product of the historical process which, as the Christian sees it, culminated in the career of Jesus and the beginnings of the Christian movement.

Now it is clear that the acceptance of such a view frees us from some of the more painful dilemmas created by the earlier more magical conception and greatly aids the church in its apologetic task. It prepares us perfectly to understand and without any misgiving to accept the presence in the Bible of all the features which caused such embarrassment to defenders of the older position—outmoded world view, inconsistencies, historical inaccuracies, low moral standards, and all the rest. No human group is free from fault and error, and if the Bible is the reflection and record of the life of a historical community, we shall not expect it to be free from them. If there is supreme greatness in the Bible, it is there because something supremely great had happened within the life of the community which produced it; if there are error, smallness, and even sin in the Bible, they are there because error, smallness, and sin were to be found among the people whose corporate life is reflected in it.

Perhaps it will be useful to cite one example of the practical value of recognizing this fact about the Bible—an example which will also serve as an illustration of the way the principle of interpretation we are discussing actually works out.

Just before the Second World War a new edition in Germany of the Gospel of John was described in the

American press as "nazified" because it created the impression that its author, if not Jesus himself, was a hater of the Jews. Being on the staff of the *Christian Century* at the time, I was asked to write an editorial on the report of the appearance of the new edition. I called my editorial "The Nazis Discover John" and ventured to suggest that if the ascription of Nazi influence was based only on the anti-Semitic tendency of the book, it might be appropriate to ask if the version was in reality "nazified" or merely accurate, since there can be little doubt that the author of the Fourth Gospel falls more than a little short of having what we should regard as a worthy or Christian attitude toward the Jews. And this strain of anti-Semitism, although by no means as conspicuous, is not absent from the other gospels.

Needless to say, this anti-Jewish bias cannot be attributed to Jesus. Jesus himself was a Jew—a Jew in every sense of the term, in his blood, his culture, and his religion; a Jew who never once thought of himself as anything else, who never for a moment surrendered his loyalty to Jewish institutions, who hardly stepped outside of Jewish territory. But the Christian movement which stemmed from his career did not stay long on Jewish soil. Almost at once it moved out into the Greco-Roman world, and it soon became evident that it was among Gentiles that its destiny lay. The Jewish nation by and large rejected the apostolic message. The field of evangelization was the Gentile world, and in that world the Jewish connection of the religious movement

75

was, in areas at least, a handicap. The task of the Christian evangelists and missionaries, then, was to commend to Gentiles a despised Jew who, as if that by itself were not enough, had been put to death as a criminal by an important Roman official. The tendency to mitigate or qualify the Jewishness of Jesus and to absolve the Roman executioner was under the circumstances inevitable, and the process was tremendously accelerated by the mutual opposition of synagogue and church which early existed in local communities throughout the Roman Empire. The gospels were written in this atmosphere of Jewish-Christian hostility.

Its effect upon the tradition appears in the most primitive gospel, Mark, where as early as the third chapter the Pharisees are represented as conspiring to destroy Jesus. It is enormously important in Matthew, with its bitter invective against the Pharisees (the terrible "Woes") and its ascription to the whole Jewish nation of that most horrible of all curses, "His blood be on us and on our children!"—a justifying in advance of all the anti-Jewish persecutions of all the Christian centuries. It appears in less harsh but no less unmistakable manifestation in Luke-Acts. And most of all, as we have seen, it appears in John.

History probably does not furnish another example of so complete and swift a reversal within a tradition of the facts upon which the tradition is based. A Jew crucified by the Gentiles becomes in effect a non-Jew put to death by the Jews. This reversal had already been accomplished when the Fourth Gospel was written at the end of the first century.

This fact gives rise to two reflections among others. For one thing the Christian is forced to remember again the unspeakable crimes which have been committed against the Jews during the last fifteen centuries in the name of Christ, and to recognize moreover with humility and penitence that the classic and normative documents of Christianity have in some measure aided and abetted in their perpetration. But the second reflection is the immediately relevant one. Here is a conspicuous example of the value, even the necessity, of the historical approach to the New Testament documents. The anti-Semitic strain in the gospels brings home again the fact that the New Testament grew out of the experiences of the early church, that it reflects the message of Jesus and the meaning of Christ through the lives of men and women who understood perhaps as imperfectly as we still do the great thing they were trying to interpret. The marks of their sin, as well as of their ignorance, lie upon their work. The gospels are not to be looked at but to be looked through, and one cannot do this adequately until one is ready and able to allow accurately for the defects of the medium. To say that this is especially true of the Gospel of John is not to discount the value and significance of what is in many ways the New Testament's supreme book and the crowning achievement of early Christian interpretative genius and art.

The anti-Semitism of the gospels is only one of many

77

features presenting difficulties for the apologist which the use of historical method enables him to meet adequately and without embarrassment. Inconsistencies in narrative among the different gospels, divergencies in the ways Jesus' words are reported, anachronisms of various kinds—these are other features of which detractors of Christianity were once able to make devastating use. It is the wide acceptance of the historical method in biblical study which has rendered the Ingersolls of another generation irrelevant, impotent, and for the most part silent.

II

But to return to our major question: Granted that historical biblical criticism has been valuable in apologetic, has it enriched, or is it capable of enriching, the church's own life? By way of general answer to this question it may be pointed out that the basic ground for the appropriateness, the religious and theological value, of historical method in the study of the Bible lies in the essential nature of Christianity as a historical religion. Over and over again in these pages it has been affirmed that the revelation of God in Christ was God's action in and through a historical event—an event which issued in, and in a sense is perpetuated in, a historical community, but which in another sense transcends the community and provides the norm of its continuing life. It is necessary to reaffirm and to emphasize again this same fact, because if it is not true, the whole idea of this chapter, as

78

indeed of this book, collapses. On the other hand if the affirmation is true, the value of historical method is established, for only by this method can any historical event be recovered. By the "recovery" of a historical event at least four things are meant: (1) the discernment of it as a definite and distinguishable entity, having its own distinctive character and force; (2) the analysis of it as regards the various factors which created it and the various stages in its development; (3) the apprehension of it as rooted firmly in history; and (4) the imaginative grasping of it as a concrete whole. The value of "recovering" the event Jesus Christ in all four of these senses will hardly be disputed. One may have greater doubt that the historical method is an indispensable or even a useful tool. Responsibility for this doubt must be charged in no small part to the historical critics themselves, who have often misunderstood and misused their own method; but the method itself not only does not carry any threat to precious values but offers us new riches of understanding which are otherwise inaccessible and unattainable.

First of all, then, the application of historical method is essential to the establishment of the event in its true and distinct integrity. The importance of maintaining the distinction between event and church was discussed in the preceding chapter. It was pointed out that the blurring of this distinction, which has the effect of making the continuing church the norm of its own life, is the basic Roman Catholic error—an error which the

Protestant seeks to correct by placing the church under the authority of the Bible. But actually it is not what was written that has authority, but what happened. The Bible has value only because it brings us a firsthand account of that happening. The event is the important thing, not the account; and we must *interpret* the account to recover the event. This interpretation goes on inevitably and constantly whether we know it or not. It goes on, however skillfully or ineptly, however truly or falsely.

The Roman Church has by and large been more clearly and consistently aware of this necessity of interpretation than has Protestantism, as well as more sensitive to the dangers implicit in it. Those dangers are of course subjectivism and individualism. If scripture must in the nature of the case be interpreted, any authority it has must be its authority as interpreted; and if every individual is free to interpret it as seems best to him, it ceases to have authority at all. As against this contingency the Roman Church takes its firm and characteristic stand: the Bible has authority only as it is interpreted by the church.

Now it is important to recognize both the truth in this position as thus stated and also the degree to which all Christians share it. It has been urged again and again in these pages that the scriptures are the product of the church's life and can be understood only within the context which that life provides. The Roman Catholic is mistaken in so far as he identifies the church with his own hierarchy; but he is not mistaken in putting the church above the individual and in insisting on the decisive part the church must have in the interpretation of scripture. The Protestant on the other hand is not mistaken in emphasizing the role of the Spirit in the interpretation of scripture and in preferring the voice of the Spirit to the vote of some bishops, but he is badly mistaken if he supposes that when he speaks of the Spirit, he is not also speaking of the church. What is the church but the people of the Spirit? What is the Spirit in the Christian's experience but the breath of the church, the creative and sustaining principle of its life? The Spirit is of course the Holy Spirit, God's own Spirit, and therefore is more than the church; but he is also the Spirit of Christ and therefore can be known only within the community of Christ. Any other "spirit" than that which belongs indigenously and essentially to the church—to the church as the embodiment of this community—is not the Spirit, the Spirit of Christian experience and faith. The Protestant may often be mistaken in his identification of this Spirit and in his understanding of what the Spirit says, just as the Roman Catholic, being mistaken in his identification of the church, is often mistaken in his hearing of what the church says; but it cannot be that the Spirit shall say one thing to us and the church (truly understood) another. The voice of the church (in the true sense of the term) and the voice of the Spirit are one voice, and there can be no question about the decisive role of this voice in the interpretation of

81

scripture. For both Catholic and Protestant a large part of the authority of the Bible is authority with which the church invests it. Although the Catholic has been more ready to see this than the Protestant, it is true for both.

But it is not the whole truth. It is not the whole truth for the reason emphasized in the preceding chapter. Despite the close and inseparable connection between the event and the community the ultimate norm in Christianity is not the community but the event. The integrity of the event as in some sense and degree distinguishable from and normative for the community must be maintained. The value of the scriptures has been found in their bringing us a firsthand account of this event. But if the scriptures are to be interpreted simply and only in the light of the church's continuing experience or by the authority of its self-perpetuating hierarchy, the event is on the way to losing its integrity and its authority.

It was urged in the second and third chapters of this book that historical method cannot "hurt" us by destroying our memory of the event in its essential character and significance. It may now be seen that what is substantially this same danger really threatens us—but from a very different quarter. The real peril lies in the tendency, characteristic of both Christian piety and Christian ecclesiasticism, to absorb the event completely within the continuing life of the church. The only way of escape is through the attempt to apprehend the event in its original character and impact. This is the biblical historian's enterprise, and the only conceivable method is his method. Although many Protestants have not seen it yet, it is still true that to maintain in any important degree the autonomy of the event and its precedence to the church commits them to the use of the only method by which the event in its distinctness and integrity can with maximum fullness and truth be identified and recovered.

III

Historical method in the second place assists us in the "recovery" of the event by enabling us to distinguish, as far as this is possible, the various factors which created it and the various stages in its development—to recognize the dynamic character and the inner complexity of the event.

Whatever our conception of the primary locus of revelation (and so long as we recognize the close and intricate interrelationship between event, church, and Bible, each of the three possible conceptions of this locus is at least approximately true), it is both inevitable and proper that we should want to understand this medium of revelation as fully as we can. If it is thought of as an event, we are bound to ask such questions as, How did it begin? How did it progress? When, and how, and why did this or that happen? As we have noted several times, questions like these are not the most important questions that can be asked; more especially, no conceivable difference of opinion among historians on matters of this kind poses any threat whatever to any vital interest

83

of Christian faith. But who will deny the value of as clear an understanding as we can attain of the historical event upon which we are so dependent? Such understanding involves inevitably the use of historical method. The disinterested seeking of such understanding is precisely what historical method is.

Particularly valuable for the understanding of the event and the interpretation of the New Testament is the discernment of the way in which fact and interpretation of fact interacted with each other as the event occurred and are related to each other in the event as a whole. This objective-subjective character of the event (as indeed of any historical event) has been emphasized before and will be further stressed and illustrated in the following chapter. In the present connection it will be enough to point out that only if one is seeking the event beyond the New Testament as the object of greatest concern is one able to give free and full recognition to the variety of the New Testament itself.

If it is believed that God has revealed himself simply in the words of the scriptures as such, there is no way of tolerating discrepancy (and we are mistaken if we suppose there can be variety in a matter of this kind without discrepancy). One is forced, for example, to deny any essential differences among the gospels. One cannot sharply distinguish between the thought of Paul and, say, the thought of the Epistle to the Hebrews; it is on this account that fundamentalists find it possible to suppose that Paul wrote Hebrews. Even works so disparate as

Revelation and the Fourth Gospel can be attributed to the same author. Indeed all of the books of the New Testament are really attributed to the same author—namely, to God himself. Therefore harmony is an a priori necessity, and the sharp edges of the biblical books are blurred, their distinctive notes muted, their characteristic structures and shapes obscured or distorted.

Only recognition of the dynamic character of God's revelation in Christ—that is, that it took place, not in a static book, but in a living, moving event—can free us not only to accept the rich variety of New Testament religion, with all the discrepancies which genuine variety always involves, but to welcome it gratefully and joyously. These disparate voices are all bearing witness to an event whose concrete meaning far surpassed the power of any words, categories, or myths fully to express it, but which can be apprehended the more adequately because so many attempts were made and were made so differently.

But the true unity of the New Testament may also be more clearly seen. That unity does not consist either in the uniformity of the parts or in the nice mechanical adjustment of part to part; it is an organic unity corresponding to the unity of the dynamic event which it records and reflects. By placing the documents in approximate chronological order, as only historical study makes possible, one may trace the gradual deepening and widening of the church's first realization of the meaning of the event and thus the gradual unfolding of the event itself—for the event had not fully occurred until this initial process of realization was complete.

Only on the basis of such an analysis can one distinguish with the maximum of precision and truth between the essential and the nonessential elements in the event. By "essential" are meant those elements which not only were actually present in it but could not conceivably have been lacking. Without them the event would not have been itself. Not all actual elements in the event can be said to have this structural character. The anti-Semitism, for example, which, as we have seen, developed in certain parts at least of the primitive church, was existentially a phase of the event—perhaps, as things were, a necessary phase. But it certainly was not an essential phase; that is, it was not implicit in or required by the structure of the event; indeed it represents a distortion. Such judgments as between essential and nonessential, or between less and more important, elements in the event are inescapable and are made, even if only tacitly and unconsciously, by all readers of the New Testament. Obviously the subjective cannot be eliminated entirely from these judgments of value; but in so far as they have a sound objective ground, historical analysis must help provide it.

It may be added that the achievement of a sound objective ground for discriminations of this kind is a prerequisite of Christian unity. So long as Christians or bodies of Christians regard as essential and indispensable, and insist that others also must do so, features of the event which other Christians, perhaps the great majority, regard as accidental and irrelevant, unity is impossible. The most important corrective of such intolerance is the actual continuing life of the Christian community; the event is in substance perpetuated in the community, and what is absolutely essential in it can hardly be consistently lacking in large areas of the church over long periods. The name for this "continuing life" in its essential character is the Holy Spirit, and our narrowness is often rebuked by the manifest presence of the Spirit among those who do not "follow with us." It was thus that Peter in the Acts narrative became convinced of the falseness of a partisan view which made the racial Jewishness of Jesus and his disciples an essential and normative feature of the event (Acts 11:15-17). But it must also be recognized that the historical study of the Bible has made an important contribution to the correction of individual and sectarian aberrations, both by making us aware of the variety of the New Testament and by forcing us to find its unity at a deeper level. To discover this deeper and only real unity of the New Testament is to discover what is essential in both event and church, and thus the unity of each.

IV

Besides enabling us to distinguish more sharply between event and church and among the factors and phases of the event itself, the application of historical method to the New Testament has the effect of rooting the event more firmly in history and thus of validating its reality as event; for the first and most essential qualification of a historical event is that it belong to history. This may seem a strange claim to make for a method which has often been thought of as having precisely the opposite effect. "Surely," someone says, "the principal charge against the historical criticism of the Bible is that it has thrown doubt upon the historical accuracy of so much that the Bible records. How can you say that it has actually rooted the event more firmly in history?"

Although it is not the real answer to the question, one may point out in passing that, as regards this matter of the accuracy of the Bible, historical study has not had by any means the entirely negative results which we have often supposed. Such study has confirmed and validated fully as many biblical statements of fact as it has discredited. Of course if we approach the Bible with the assumption that it is accurate in every detail and altogether, we are alert to every doubt and denial of the critics, at the same time scarcely noticing when they consent or even confirm. (It is noticeable, however, that some who denounce the critics and their methods when the results are negative are, quite inconsistently, willing to make use of their authority on other occasions when the same methods have yielded results they like better.) If we were able to approach the historical statements of the Bible with an entirely open mind, not knowing whether they are true or not but wanting to find out, we should realize that for every fact discredited by the historical critic another is more firmly established—and, it may be added, that the facts established are by any test the more important. The major facts of the career of Jesus, for example—the character and quality of his life and teaching, his crucifixion under Pontius Pilate, the emergence of the church with its knowledge of the Resurrection and its faith in Christ the Lord—these facts are fully validated by historical study. At some points, as we have seen, the believer as such does not need this validation; but he is not simply or only the believer, and in any case he sometimes needs to persuade others. Once the presupposition of the Bible's necessary accuracy is surrendered, it can be seen that the biblical critic has given us much more in the way of assurance of fact than he has taken away.

But the statement that the historical study of the Bible has had the effect of rooting the event more firmly in history was not primarily concerned with this point, which after all is more important in apologetic than for the church's understanding of itself. We are thinking, not of the accuracy of various historical statements in the Bible, but of an actual quality of the event itself: it belongs intimately and richly to the historical process. For to call something an event is to say more than that it happened. Historicity is not a mere formal fact; it is a concrete quality. An event is an integral part of human historical experience and fully shares in the nature of that experience.

It may be objected that this is a distinction without

89

a difference: if something happens at all, obviously it happens within and as a part of man's life; and if this happening has significant effects within history, it is both proper and necessary to call it a historical event. This is certainly true, but it is possible to accept in principle such a definition of a historical event and in practice to go far indeed toward dissociating the event from any realistic human context. In so far as we make this dissociation, we are denying in substance the historicity of the event, no matter how vigorously we affirm the formal fact.

Although the analogy is not exact, the way in which formal affirmation and substantial denial can be combined is illustrated by one aspect of the history of the church's effort to define the nature of the person of Jesus, who has been taken as a symbol of the event, and in whom the whole significance of the event has been found. The earlier gospel materials take the fact of Jesus' humanity for granted, but even in them one can see the operation of a tendency to supernaturalize it and thus to qualify its genuineness. This tendency reached its culmination in Docetism, with its entire and formal rejection of the real humanity. Against this denial some of the later New Testament writers react vigorously. The writer of the Fourth Gospel, for example, affirms the humanity of Jesus with the greatest boldness, clarity, and force: "The Word was made flesh." The gospel begins with this almost blunt affirmation of the formal fact, but the actual career of Jesus which it presents is hardly a human career. Jesus is allowed to show human weakness on the physical side—he can be hungry, thirsty, and weary—but he does not share any of our intellectual, moral, or emotional limitations. His consciousness is not a human consciousness: it is not of the nature of "flesh" to be omniscient, aware of pre-existence, free from temptation, uncertainty, and doubt. The Johannine conception can be recognized as being very close to a type of Docetism which held that the divine Son of God temporarily dwelt within the body of Jesus of Nazareth but did not really identify himself with him. Indeed the author of the Fourth Gospel came as near to being a Docetist as one can come to holding in substance a position which one repudiates in principle—but it is surprising how very near this can be.

In somewhat the same way one may insist on the historicity of an event as formal fact and deny it as concrete quality. To affirm that something happened and then to define the "happening" in such a way as to detach it from history is to deny its historicity in the moment of affirming it. This denial, which is implicit in all historical fundamentalism or dogmatism, is far more important than any "negative" conclusion of a historian. When the historian ascribes some biblical story to "legend," he does so because he is taking history seriously: he cannot see a place for the incident the story tells within the historical process he is examining, but he can see a place within that process for the creation and growth of the story itself. Taken as legend, the story says something true about history; taken otherwise, it is simply incredible and meaningless. The historian may of course be mistaken in any particular case, but his method is sound. On the other hand the dogmatist who affirms that every biblical story is an accurate account of an actual incident can maintain his position only by denying in effect the truly historical character of the biblical material. He saves the mere "happenedness" of particular incidents at the expense of the true historicity of the entire event. Can there be any question as to which procedure is in the last resort the more destructive?

V

The last of the four creative contributions of biblical historical scholarship mentioned at the beginning of this chapter is its service in enabling the imagination of the church to grasp more vividly the concrete reality of the event, especially in some of its phases or parts.

This service it has performed partly by making fresh information available to us, by filling in from extra-biblical sources the background of biblical personalities, happenings, and ideas. The Bible itself does not provide sufficient material for that graphic understanding of its contents which, though it may not be indispensable, is obviously desirable and valuable. How eager we are, for example, actually to visualize the life of Jesus! And yet the gospels give us no adequate basis for a real picture. They bring us a meager selection of material. Much even of this tells us more about the primitive church—

its needs, activities, interests, and faith—than about Jesus himself. But even if all of the biographical material could be accepted at face value, one would need to recognize that it covers at most only two or three years of Jesus' career and is concerned only with what proved to be its most significant aspects. How are we to fill in the enormous lacunae?

The answer is that at many points we cannot do so and probably shall never be able to do so (nor of course do we need to). But then after acknowledging the meagerness of our information, we remember that the life of Jesus was the life of a Jew in Galilee in the first century and realize that our knowledge is richer than we thought. We are accustomed to saying that the gospels are our only substantial sources for the life of Jesus; in the obvious sense that is true. But in another sense everything, literary or archeological, which throws light upon life in Palestine at the beginning of our era helps illuminate the life of Jesus. Without this light the human career of Jesus is either an abstraction or a modernization. If we "see" his life at all (that is, visualize it concretely), we do so either with approximate truth in the light which the historian makes available to us or else naïvely and falsely in terms of our own experience. This can be said also of the life of Paul and the beginnings of the church as Acts and the epistles record them.

Essentially the same point can be made about some of the distinctive biblical ideas, although the term "visualize" does not apply. What meaning did the term "Son of

93

Man" have in Jesus' teaching, or the word *logos* in the prologue of the Fourth Gospel? Naïve Christian experience does not provide true answers to such questions. One is able to feel the original force of such conceptions and to understand their appeal only through acquaintance with the cultural milieux to which they belong. And only historical method applied to the literary and archaeological materials, biblical and nonbiblical, can help us gain this familiarity.

But we are already thinking of more than the mere giving of fresh information, the imparting of new facts. The use of historical method opens the way to deeper insight into the concrete meaning of the facts, new and old. If this service is not generally recognized, the cause is certainly in part the failure of biblical scholars to realize this potential value of their method. Biblical historical scholarship, like historical scholarship generally, has often limited itself to the ascertaining of facts, with a consequent disregard of meanings and values. This self-limitation is a phase of the devotion to objectivity which has been characteristic of modern historiography. External facts can be established, it is thought, impersonally and scientifically; the assertion of meanings and values rests ultimately upon personal and necessarily somewhat subjective grounds. The historian, who in modern times has tended to regard himself more as a scientist than as an artist or philosopher, has sought to avoid committing himself on such matters. But there is a growing recognition among historians, biblical and other, that although

94

one thus escapes certain risks of subjective error, one also misses the chance of really knowing the truth. For history, the object of the historian's study, is itself a compound of fact and meaning. <u>The historian must not only be critical; he must also be creative.</u> He must not only "get down" to the facts of his subject; he must also reach up to its meaning. The historian may often fail to "rise" to this meaning, and as a consequence his work may be dry, lifeless, and irrelevant; but freed from an artificial preoccupation with bare facts, the historian has <u>the opportunity and the competence to enter imaginatively into the real meaning of any epoch or event</u> in a degree altogether beyond the capacity of other men equally gifted.

A poet, or a philosopher, or a saint may in a given case be able to grasp the real meaning of a historical event better than a particular historian. But to the historian who is also poet, philosopher, or saint possibilities of understanding are open to which no saint, philosopher, or poet who is not a historian could conceivably attain.

VI

To say this is to say that there is possible in the modern period a deeper, fuller, and more creative understanding of the Bible than was ever possible before. The church has always had its philosophers and poets and saints, but the historian, as his function and method are now understood, is a fairly recent arrival. The recognition of this fact is itself enough to prevent our attaching too high

95

a value to his work: after all, Christian devotion was able to exist for many centuries without him, and the scriptures yielded their treasures of life to the millions who searched them, albeit without his guidance and his tools. To be sure, the modern age which produced him also produced intellectual problems which we can scarcely solve without his help, so that in apologetic he comes nearer to being indispensable. But it remains true that the biblical historical scholar (even when his help in apologetic is taken into account) is not essential to the continuing life of the church, but neither for that matter is the philosopher or poet. Only the saint is really essential. But this fact must not be permitted to blind us to the many and great services which the historian and only the historian can render—such services as we have considered in this chapter.

It is understandable that the church, which managed so long without him, should now wonder sometimes whether she needs him. Besides he has often actually functioned in such a way as to make it appear that if Christian faith and devotion were to flourish, it could be only in spite of him—certainly not in any degree because of him. But this failure is the failure and misfortune of youth and will be overcome. As the church learns to set the biblical historian free and as the historian learns that he can be truly free only in her service, he will not only furnish the church with ever-mightier weapons in her defense but will enrich her with new treasures of truth and life.

96

CHAPTER VI

Historical Criticism and Preaching

IN the preceding pages an attempt has been made to evaluate the bearing of biblical historical criticism upon Christian faith. Because of the complexity, almost the contradictoriness, of the relationship the undertaking is not a simple or easy one. On the one hand we must recognize the unique and all but indispensable services which historical method can render and in a degree has rendered both to Christian apologetic and to the church's own devotion and self-understanding. On the other hand we must not so overestimate the importance of the historian as to make him the arbiter of Christian life and faith. We are not as Christians in the position of looking wistfully to the historian to see whether we can continue to be Christians or not. We are not under the necessity of saying to the historian at any vital point, "By your leave, sir." At the same time only with great loss could we dispense with his services.

97

Without undertaking any further advance in the theoretical development of our theme, let us now attempt a practical application. How does the understanding of biblical criticism which we have been considering bear upon the work of the preacher?

I

The whole problem with which this book has been engaged comes to rather sharp focus at this point because both the biblical historian and the preacher are interpreters of the Bible. They are both teachers by profession, and teachers of the same subject material and to a considerable degree of the same pupils. Any discrepancy between them as to the meaning of that subject material, especially if it is concerned with so basic a matter as the method to be used in the study of it, not only cannot be hidden or minimized, but is certain to be a source of serious confusion and division within the church. No one will deny that such discrepancy has often existed. The teacher's desk and the preacher's pulpit—two separate worlds! The lecture and the sermon—two separate realms of discourse!

Some of the responsibility for this separateness can be attributed to obvious defects in the preacher and the scholar. The preacher has sometimes been more concerned to use the Bible than to interpret it—that is, he has come to the Bible seeking not a sermon but a text for a sermon, asking not, "What shall I preach?" but, "What shall I preach on?" He seizes on words of scripture which seem to suit his own purposes and uses them without reference to their true meaning or original intention. Whatever justification may be possible for occasional resort to homiletical tricks of this kind—and if the congregation is fully "let in" on the tricks, they do not need to be actually dishonest—no one would defend this kind of thing as being the interpretation of scripture. As a persistent practice it represents a basically frivolous attitude toward the Bible and is unworthy of the preacher. On the other hand, as we have seen (pages 18-20), equally lacking in seriousness is the biblical scholarship which exhausts itself in solving various linguistic, literary, and historical puzzles or which devotes itself entirely to what it calls "facts," disregarding meanings and values. No wonder such preachers and such scholars cannot get together! But these are not the majority in either category. And our problem in this final chapter is the problem often created for the serious biblical preacher by the serious biblical scholar.

There can be no doubt that many such preachers, whether they fully acknowledge it or not, think of the critic as their "natural enemy." Their business is to preach the gospel, and the Bible, especially the New Testament, is their major source and resource; but it would appear that the critics' business is, if not the reducing of the gospel, certainly the reducing of the available material to be used in preaching it. "He does not leave us much to preach!" is a comment I have often heard on one or another of the more radical biblical critics. Does it need to be urged again that this attitude, though understandable, is inappropriate and mistaken? It is true that the lower or textual critics occasionally take away a word or a phrase or even a sentence from some received text, but textual criticism is approved and its results accepted even by the fundamentalists. As for the so-called higher criticism, it cannot destroy a single word in the gospels. The entire New Testament stands as an eyewitness account of the event the proclamation of which *is* the gospel, and no historical criticism can either reduce its contents or impair its authenticity and truth. Criticism seems to many to have this impairing effect largely because of at least three false preconceptions which have been touched on elsewhere in this book, but which need to be mentioned again in the present connection.

II

One of these misconceptions is the identification of authenticity with apostolic authorship. The grounds for the original emphasis upon authorship by apostles were briefly discussed in some earlier remarks about the canon. It was seen that this criterion was settled on as being a manageable test of nearness to the normative event. But once we see that it is this nearness which is the really important thing, why should we continue to set such high store by what is obviously a merely approximate measure? And yet we do. There are not many circles within the church where discussion of the question of authorship as regards, say, Ephesians or I Peter can be carried on in an atmosphere entirely free from religious or theological bias. We are likely to approach and to deal with such a question as though we were being forced into the position of questioning the good faith of an old and tried friend.

But truth and authenticity as well as greatness in a document are not dependent upon authorship; we know that well enough everywhere else but in the Bible. The Epistle to the Ephesians is one of the greatest and most authentic documents in the New Testament— authentic in the sense of being a true and firsthand setting forth of the meaning of the event—without the slightest reference to whether Paul wrote it or not. We may go further and say that Ephesians is an authentic *Pauline* document—in the sense of embodying characteristic Pauline ideas—but even this is true regardless of authorship. We may argue that Paul wrote it because it is Pauline; we cannot argue that it is Pauline because Paul wrote it. The authenticity of the document—as primitive Christian or even as Pauline—is simply not involved in the question of authorship. The belief that the Epistle to the Hebrews was written by Paul would not in a thousand years make that a Pauline document; as a matter of fact that belief, made universal and binding by ecclesiastical decree, had something more than a thousand years in which to try to do this, but it finally failed. On the other hand no apostolic name is needed to establish the authenticity of Hebrews as a fresh, significant,

101

and true interpretation of the event as it first occurred and was first understood. But what apostolic name could conceivably make Titus or II Peter really function in the church as creative or normative works? What real use do even those who still maintain the apostolic authorship of these documents, sometimes almost with violence (and indeed it requires violence to maintain such views) —what use do even they actually make of these books in their preaching?

"But," someone says, "you are disregarding the significance of the claims biblical documents often make for themselves. When a book represents itself as being the work of an apostle, how can we question its authorship without questioning also its authenticity? In the case of anonymous works like Hebrews and the Fourth Gospel it may well be argued that only a certain supposed prestige is involved in the question of authorship. But Ephesians claims Paul as its author, and I Peter claims Peter. How can these documents be regarded as authentic if these identifications are false?"

The answer is that here again the test is intrinsic. Pseudonymity was widely practiced in the ancient world and with a great variety of motives. It might be used as a mere literary device, being understood and accepted as such by the readers of the work. It might be resorted to because the actual author felt himself to be so indebted to his master in what he had written that to attach his own name to his work would have seemed immodest, ungrateful, and dishonest. It might be used because the

102

whole purpose of the work was to set forth the thought of the one in whose name it was written. On the other hand the pseudonymous writer's motive might be more questionable: he wanted to secure for what he believed to be true and important a wider and more serious reading than his own name would assure. But even here our moral judgment upon his act will depend somewhat on how unselfish or selfish we think his aims were, and on whether we decide he sincerely believed the ideas he expressed to be those of the writer whose name he used or find ourselves forced to conclude that he was guilty of a deliberate forgery. It must be granted that if a work is proved to be such a forgery, it can hardly be called authentic; but the major element in the "proof" will be the inauthenticity (otherwise established) of the work. Neither I Peter nor Ephesians is a forgery, whoever wrote it. We know it is not a forgery because of the general character of the book; whatever the reason for the adoption of pseudonymity it could not have been a selfish desire to deceive. The quality of the work precludes that possibility. As much cannot be said for II Peter, but here too one must not be too quick to say that the only alternatives are Petrine authorship and forgery.

In a word, we ought to judge the character of the pseudonymity by the character of the book in each case, not the character of the book by the mere fact of pseudonymity. No derogation of the value and authority of a biblical book is involved in any ascription of pseudonym-

103

ity or in any other view we may take of its authorship. We may well question this value and authority in a given case (as Luther did not hesitate to do in the case of the Epistle of James), but always on more intrinsic grounds—and the question is as likely to be raised by the preacher as by the historical scholar.

A second misconception which often plagues the preacher in his relations with the biblical historian is the assumption that to explain a happening, as far as one can, in terms of natural causes and sequences is in effect to deny that it can have any great significance; in other words, that to understand is to despise. This false assumption is often apparently shared by the scholar himself. "Oh, I know how that happened," he says and proceeds to cite influences and pressures from this side and that with the proud air of one who supposes that he is destroying the fact or at least any significance it may have by explaining it. Now it would not be hard to demonstrate that no explanation does more than scratch the surface of even the least important concrete fact—as Tennyson's "Flower in the Crannied Wall" will remind us. But even if our explanations of a historical event could be more adequate, they still would not place in the slightest jeopardy either the reality of the event or the significance it has proved to have within the history of a people or a culture.

So far as the event Jesus Christ is concerned, the important thing to remember is that its significance inheres in the event as a whole rather than in any specific factor or feature of it. The meaning of the whole is not the resultant of the meanings of the several parts but the source of those meanings. A significant historical event is, as we have already noted, not a mechanical aggregate but a living unity. The historian dealing with causations and factors, like the botanist analyzing seeds and soils, is making a contribution to our understanding; but the concrete reality of the event, like that of the plant, is untouched by his analysis, and the ultimate mystery of its being cannot be impaired.

A historical scholar, for example, seeks to explain the fact of Jesus' crucifixion. He describes the political situation in Palestine in the first century; he presents his views as to the political bearing, or the supposed political bearing, of Jesus' teachings; he identifies Jesus' enemies and persuasively formulates the reasons for their hostility. Thus in a sense he "explains" the crucifixion. But the meaning of the death of Christ within the Christian church, although it may be at certain points enriched by these findings, could not conceivably be impoverished by them and for the most part is untouched by them. For that meaning rests, not upon a consideration of causes and factors, but upon the church's experience of the entire event—Jesus' life, death, resurrection, the coming into being of the church—one indivisible whole. The situation is not that the event has significance because of the significance of the death, but rather that the death has significance because of the significance of the event.

This significance no historical explanation of the crucifixion can imperil or reduce.

To say this is to come close to stating the third and most important of the three misconceptions we are considering. This is the identification of the event with what is in fact only a part of the event—namely, with the so-called historical facts which emerge from the researches of the scholars.

The Christian gospel is the good news that something has happened which not only sets the meaning of human life in a new light but also makes available a new forgiveness, healing, righteousness, and peace—in a word, a new salvation. To preach is to proclaim this good news, developing, as far as possible, its countless implications, opening up, as one is able, the whole vast and varied wealth of its meaning. But what is this "something" that happened? It began (in the approximate sense in which alone an event can ever be said to begin) with the appearance of a Jewish teacher; it ended (in the same approximate sense) with the clear and full emergence into history of a dynamic community within whose experience the reality of God was known in a new and characteristic way. What lies between this beginning and end is "the event," and, as we have often seen, there can be no possible question as to its having happened.

The scholar is often occupied in trying to distinguish between the outer or bare facts of Jesus' career and the beginnings of the church on the one hand, and the meanings these facts had for the early Christians on the other; between what happened in the public eye and what happened in the community's experience. This occupation, as we saw in the last chapter, is not a mere academic exercise but has importance for the Christian theological enterprise. But any scholar thus occupied who supposes that the distinction he is making is between the event on the one hand and what does not belong to the event on the other is mistaken, as is any preacher who makes the same assumption. The event is by definition something that happened, not primarily on the stage of Jewish or Roman history (as a matter of fact little happened there, as the virtual silence of Jewish and Roman historians bears witness), but within the life of the Christian community. And that "something that happened" must be taken as a whole—fact and meaning, two equally important elements in this as in every other event, inseparable and only partly distinguishable, inextricably involved with each other in a concrete organic whole.

The historian may offer convincing reasons for the opinion that a given item in the New Testament reflects the primitive church's understanding of a fact which probably appeared to others quite differently. But what of that? It is precisely the church's understanding in which we are interested. That understanding entered creatively into the development of the event which we proclaim; the appearance of the same fact to others had no significant social effects at all, did not become a part of history in any sense, and certainly is of subordinate

107

interest to the Christian preacher. His way of using such an item will, to be sure, be somewhat different because he has read the historian and accepted his view as to its original character; but there is no reason why he should not use it. The historian has not necessarily lowered its status or lessened its authority; he has not detached or removed it from the event. On the contrary he has defined its place within the event more sharply and accurately, and thus has located it there if possible more surely and firmly than before.

III

It has just been said that a preacher conversant with the work of the biblical historian and convinced of the soundness of his method will actually use the biblical material in a somewhat different way. What is that "different way"? It can be illustrated more effectively than it can be defined, and some illustrations will be offered later in this chapter. Meantime, however, a few remarks of a more general nature may be appropriate.

The question can be a very poignant one. In my own experience it is an unusual seminary class in New Testament in which more than once someone does not ask, obviously with deep concern, "How can we use this in preaching?" or, "What can we say about this to our people?" On the one hand the minister wants to be honest; on the other he knows how shocking and destructive the results of the literary and historical criticism of the Bible can sometimes appear. Just how can he steer his course so as to escape both obscurantism and negativism?

The chances are that a preacher who raises the question in this form has not fully assimilated biblical criticism and in particular that he has not seen the positive, creative values of the historical method. He is afraid of its destructive effects upon his congregation because he is himself a sufferer from those same effects. He is a victim of the misconceptions we have been considering in this chapter. So long as this is true, there is no escape from his dilemma. He cannot avoid either obscurantism or negativism because for him there is no third alternative. He cannot give to others light which he has not received.

On the other hand to stand in this light is the greater part of knowing how to share it. The interpreter of the Bible for whom historical method has positive and creative meaning and results will probably not be greatly troubled by the problem of how to apply the method in his preaching in a positive and creative way. He will do so inevitably with assurance and authority—and, it may be added, with a minimum of harmful shock to those who hear him.

Such an interpreter will see the so-called negative findings of biblical criticism in true perspective and thus will see that they are neither as important nor as negative as they may seem to others. Therefore he neither emphasizes nor ignores them; he neither hails, denounces, nor avoids. The modernist preacher who, taking a text from Hebrews, insists vehemently and with all the arguments that Paul

109

did not write that epistle and the fundamentalist preacher who insists with the same vehemence (though necessarily with fewer arguments) that Paul did write it are exactly alike, and are equally mistaken, in their basic presupposition: both of them see the question of the Pauline authorship of Hebrews as having an importance it does not have. But the same mistake is being made also by the third preacher who carefully avoids giving his congregation any inkling of his opinion on the subject. All of them show that they regard the denial of Pauline authorship as having important negative implications. The modernist rejoices in these implications and declares that Paul did not write Hebrews with the air of one who thinks it is his principal duty to disabuse people's minds of traditional historical errors. The fundamentalist abhors these implications and declares that Paul did write Hebrews with the air of a defender of the faith. The true interpreter accepts the fact of non-Pauline authorship without either embarrassment or fanfare because its implications do not seem to him very important or ultimately negative. The same thing can be said about his attitude toward the scholar's answers to other more significant or more controversial historical questions.

The minister who thus understands and assimilates the results of the historical study of the Bible can hardly fail over the years to impart to the members of his congregation a new conception of the meaning and proper use of the Bible. This new conception will have replaced the old gradually and largely imperceptibly. The change will have occurred, not because the minister has either attacked the old or defended the new—the theoretical issue may never have been raised—but because over and over again he has made the Bible, *looked at in his way,* become alive and relevant and more deeply significant than it had been before.

IV

It has been more than once hinted, if not affirmed, in this chapter that, far from taking resources away from the preacher of the gospel, the historical study of the Bible has made richer resources available to him; that, historically understood, the Bible provides him with not "less to preach" but "more to preach." To attempt a practical demonstration of the truth of that statement would seem to be an appropriate way to conclude the discussion of preaching and the whole book. Our examples will be taken from the gospels, where historical method is likely to be most distrusted, and will represent some at least of the kinds of material where, it has often been held, the historical critic has most discouraged and hampered the homiletical interpreter. We shall deal first with some stories upon whose "historicity" the historian has thrown doubt, second with a saying of Jesus whose "authenticity" he has questioned, and third with a more pervasive teaching of the gospels whose original meaning and intention, as the historian asks us to understand them, have at least to some extent proved untrue.

In all three of the Synoptic Gospels the first reference to Jesus' impressive teaching (in Matthew and Luke rather full accounts of the teaching are given) is followed by a number of narratives which set forth Jesus' miraculous powers. The Gospel of Luke brings us at this point the stories of the healing of the centurion's slave (7:2-10), the raising of the son of the widow of Nain (7:11-17), the stilling of the storm (8:22-25), the cleansing of the Gerasene demoniac (8:26-39), and several other similar stories. All have parallels or equivalents in the other Synoptic Gospels.

A number of questions can be asked about any one of these narratives—for example: To what extent, if at all, is this story the account of an actual incident? How early is it known to have been in circulation in the church? Why was it remembered and prized? Why was it believed? What made it significant? What use was made of it in the preaching and teaching of the primitive church?

Now many a preacher—and for that matter many a historian—has believed that among these questions only one is really important, namely the first: Did this actually happen? As regards this question it is important to note that the dogmatic denial that any miracle could happen is as inadmissible as the dogmatic assertion that every miracle did happen. The question, like all questions of historical fact, can be answered only on the basis of the evidence bearing on each particular case and therefore, in the last resort, must be answered tentatively. The truth is, however, that this is the least important question in the series. Next above it in importance is the question about the date of earliest circulation. But most important, indeed alone really important, are the other questions, those concerned with the meaning the story had in the primitive church. This is true for the reason which has so often been stated in these pages: that to understand the New Testament (whether one is a historian or a preacher) is to understand the event, and the event occurred within the life of the primitive church, whose experience is integrally a part of it. Just as the very reality of light includes the experience of seeing it, so the reality of the event is not a bare, hypothetical, unknowable "something" which antedates and is independent of the responses it evoked in human senses, minds, and hearts, but includes these responses as an essential part of itself. No incident merely as such belongs to the event—rather the incident as experienced and interpreted. Therefore the important question about these miracle stories, as about all other stories in the gospels, is: Why were they believed, remembered, loved, and used?

The general answer to this general question is that the miracle stories were believed, remembered, and loved because the wonderful power of Christ was a present reality in the life of the community; they were used in preaching because they embodied and conveyed this reality. Consider the story of the healing of the centurion's slave. Whatever the origins of this story, however much or little in the way of a particular incident

113

lies back of it, we owe its preservation in the church and its presence in the gospels, not to any interest in this incident for its own sake (although of course there was some of this), but to the fact that the story so wonderfully corresponded and corresponds to the realities of the Christian's experience. Jesus is still able to save. He is absent from us in the flesh as he was from this slave, yet for us too he has only to "say the word" and our lives are made whole.

Or take the following story—the account of the raising from the dead of the son of the widow of Nain. Historical scholars are accustomed to pointing to many parallels to this story, from the Old Testament as well as from other ancient lore. One cannot read these without recognizing at least the possibility that this narrative (and the same thing can be said of many others) represents a type of story which circulated widely in the ancient world and was associated with various historical and legendary figures. But again the important question (for preaching as also for history) is not whether this incident occurred just so (this we cannot know), but what the story meant to the primitive church. There can be no doubt what that meaning was: Christ has risen from the dead and has given even now to those who believe in him a new and endless life. He has raised us to eternal life from the death of sin. This meaning is made quite explicit in the Fourth Gospel's account of a similar miracle: "I am the resurrection and the life; he who believes in me, though he die, yet shall he live, and who-

114

ever lives and believes in me shall never die." (John 11:25-26.) This is not said in so many words by Mark, Matthew, or Luke when they tell of Jesus' raising of the dead; but we entirely misunderstand them if we suppose that they are not thinking some such thoughts.

The same kind of thing can be said about the narrative of the stilling of the storm. There can be no question that the story was told and retold in the church, not primarily because it seemed to prove something about Jesus' historical career (Christians had no need of this proof, and pagans would have been only moderately impressed by it), but because it said something currently true about the power of Christ to steady us in time of danger and to rescue us from any real peril to the soul. We are to fear not even the power of nature, for wind and sea belong ultimately to him. All things are ours—both death and life—for we are Christ's. It is not unlikely that most often the story was thought of as applying to the situation of the church in the midst of a hostile world. The church is a very small ship being tossed about on "raging waves." But Christ is in the boat, and he is not asleep. He will bring the ship to port. "Take heart," he says on another similar occasion, "it is I; have no fear." (Mark 6:50.)

To understand these stories in this way is not, it is important to observe, to allegorize them; one is practicing the soberest kind of exegesis. Perhaps the early church did some allegorizing—indeed undoubtedly it did, elsewhere if not here—but if its allegorizing in a particular case

115

helped determine the structure of the story or accounts for its survival and its presence in the gospels, then the historical interpreter cannot exclude it. He is seeking the meaning of the story, and that meaning is its meaning to those who first told and listened to it and determined its form. It is not "uncritical" to interpret an allegory allegorically; indeed it would be "uncritical" to interpret it in any other way. I do not mean to suggest that the three stories we have just examined are, properly speaking, allegories, or even that allegorization is the proper term to apply to the ancient process of interpretation and use which preserved them and in part produced them; but only that whatever that process was, it entered as an essential element into the creation of the gospels and that the historical interpreter must recognize it as belonging intrinsically and inseparably to the reality he is studying. The original meaning of the story is as objective as any actual incident could be and is vastly more important because it belongs to the substance of the event as no incident merely as such can be said to do. One of the great services of recent gospel criticism is that of permitting us to understand and use the gospel materials in the vital way in which they were at first understood and used, and to do so without being guilty, or being made to feel guilty, of subjective allegorization.

V

The second kind of material chosen for discussion in this chapter is those sayings of Jesus concerning whose authenticity the historical scholar gives us reason for doubt. There are many of these dubious sayings (of no saying of Jesus of course, as of no other "purely historical" datum, can one be absolutely sure); and something has already been said about the problem which they create for many believers (see above, pages 49-55). Can the preacher make use of one of the doubtful sayings? The answer—already given implicitly and now to be made explicitly and specifically—is not only that he can do so, but also that the question whether the saying is in the ordinary sense "authentic" is for most of the preacher's purposes quite irrelevant. Illustrations were taken before from the Fourth Gospel; let us now look at a passage from the Synoptics.

In the eleventh chapter of Matthew and a parallel passage in Luke we find the account of a very high tribute paid by Jesus to John the Baptist. Calling John "a prophet? Yes, . . . and more than a prophet," and going so far as to declare that an important text of scripture itself has been fulfilled in him, Jesus concludes: "Among those born of women there has risen no one greater than John the Baptist." Now in both Matthew and Luke this tribute is immediately followed with the remark, also apparently attributed to Jesus: "Yet he who is least in the kingdom of heaven is greater than he." This remark is in such striking contrast to all that precedes it that many see it as an interpolation, a pious interjection into the earlier record of Jesus' words by a scribe or a preacher who finds it intolerable that Jesus should have spoken in

117

such exalted terms of one who was not even a Christian. The fact that the phrase "kingdom of heaven" in this half-verse seems to mean "church" (as it did later but, so far as we know, not for Jesus) strongly confirms the doubt of its original place among Jesus' own words. Besides asking this question about its "authenticity," we are bound also to wonder about its truth: after all, is the least Christian a greater man than this moral giant, this prophet who was greater than any of the prophets? When the question is put in that way, the obvious answer is "No."

But that is not the right way to put the question. What the passage as a whole is concerned with is not primarily the character of a man but the significance of an event. Granted John's greatness and the truth and importance of his message, still the reason he was "more than a prophet" is that he appeared at history's climactic moment; he spoke to men "upon whom the end of the ages has come" (I Cor. 10:11). He was "more than a prophet" because his "time" was "more than a time"; it was the moment when God's final judgment and salvation were about to be revealed. John shared the greatness of the event he presaged.

But this "greater than a prophet" is less than "the least" in the church, for once the event had fully transpired, once the Spirit had been given and the new community had come into being, something so supremely great had occurred that even the least of those who stood within the new situation had privileges which the greatest of an earlier time could not have known. To be "in Christ" is to be in a relationship to God which was not a possibility before him and is not a possibility apart from him. "Blessed are your eyes, for they see, and your ears, for they hear. Truly, I say to you, many prophets and righteous men longed to see what you see, and did not see it, and to hear what you hear, and did not hear it." (Matt. 13:16-17.)

That "the time" had this kind of significance, that the life, death, and resurrection of Jesus made a difference of crucial importance, so that after that event nothing could be the same again—this is an essential element in Christian faith. The whole New Testament is an affirmation of the fact of this difference and a setting forth of its meaning. The very existence of the church bears witness to the new time; preaching is by definition the proclamation of it, and the sacraments are celebrations of its significance.

All of this being true, what can we say about the disputed saying in Matthew except that it is an authentic word of Christ? This does not mean that Jesus said it—whether he did or not does not greatly matter—but that it sets forth truly the word of God in Christ. The historian may raise or confirm a doubt in our minds as to the authenticity of the saying as an actual word of Jesus in the flesh, but when he enables us, as he does, to apprehend more vividly the way in which the first believers felt the seriousness and the significance of history and especially the portentous meaning of their own time, he

119

prepares us to recognize the authenticity of the saying in a far deeper sense and to see a place for it in the preaching of the gospel far more significant than we could have seen without his help.

VI

We turn finally to a problem of a different kind—the problem which the critic of the gospels creates for us, not by raising a doubt as to the "authenticity" of a teaching of Jesus, but by making such a doubt impossible. We have in mind here, not a single saying or even several related sayings (for the "authenticity" of separate sayings can never be established), but rather a general conception which seems to be presupposed in all Jesus' teaching—namely, the conception that history is shortly to end and the new age, the kingdom of God, is on the point of beginning. There can be no doubt that the gospels attribute such a conception to Jesus. Since this expectation was not fulfilled, we might wish that the historian would give us reason for denying that Jesus entertained it; and some critics have argued that this feature of Jesus' recorded teaching represents the thinking of the primitive church, not his own thinking. But although no one would question that many separate eschatological sayings have been colored, and some of them perhaps created, by early Christian beliefs, the great majority of critics find the evidence that Jesus expected the early end of the present age too pervasive and massive to be denied.

120

It may be pointed out in passing that not nearly so much significance as we have often imagined would belong to a shift of responsibility for this kind of teaching from Jesus to the primitive church, even if we could "bring it off." Whoever was originally responsible, it is indisputable that a vivid belief in the quick and sudden end of the age belongs integrally and decisively to the earliest phase of the history of the church. Not only do the gospels presuppose this belief, but also Paul's letters, Acts, and most of the epistles clearly reflect it. At an earlier stage in this discussion we were able to regard the anti-Semitism in the New Testament as an accretion, as "nonessential," a "distortion." This was not a purely subjective, ethically determined judgment: the anti-Semitism is limited and of relatively late origin; moreover (and this is the really decisive consideration) it is completely out of harmony with other more important elements in the New Testament and was in no sense a creative factor in the development of the event. But we cannot thus dispose of the eschatology of the New Testament. It belongs to the very warp and woof of the New Testament. It is woven into the very pattern and texture of the event. Without anti-Semitism the event would have been essentially what it was; without eschatology it would have been something essentially different. This being true, it does not greatly matter whether Jesus was personally responsible for the eschatological hopes of the first believers; these hopes in any case belonged to the event, and that is the important

121

thing. Let the possibility be granted that Jesus did not hold the eschatological ideas ascribed to him; even so, he was *understood* to hold them, and it was this understanding of his teaching (not what he may actually have taught) which entered formatively into the event, has historical importance, and possesses authority in the church. As a matter of fact, however, the historian gives us every reason to believe that the primitive church did not misunderstand Jesus at this point and that its expectation of the early end of history was his own expectation also.

But what is the modern preacher to do with this eschatological teaching? The answer is that he is to use it—to use it in the way in which historical study alone will enable him to use it, for only such study will disclose the real meaning of eschatology within the life of the primitive church. The preacher thus equipped will recognize that the eschatological teaching of the New Testament says at least three things which not only belonged ineradicably to early and normative Christianity but also are permanently true.

It speaks first of the finitude and sin of man and of the limitations of history. It stands in perpetual and emphatic denial of the whole humanistic illusion, that man can achieve his own salvation, that unlimited progress in the good life is possible within history. The kingdom of God, if it is to come, must be a new age, not a development of or even a growth out of the present one. It affirms secondly that this kingdom will come. Christian-

122

ity, for all its realism, is ultimately hopeful—hopeful not in some merely wistful sense but confidently and joyously. Love, faith, and hope abide! The form which the fulfillment of this hope will take cannot be "spelled out" in matter-of-fact terms, whether for the individual or for history; but the hope itself is inalienable and indefeasible. The eschatological teaching of the New Testament enshrines it in the only form available to its writers or the community out of which and to which they spoke; to deny, reduce, or ignore it would be to miss and to misrepresent the event of which the eschatological hope was an essential and creative part.

But most of all, the eschatological teaching of the New Testament speaks of the perpetual immediacy in Christ of God's ultimate judgment and salvation. "The kingdom of God is at hand," says the New Testament in every part from beginning to end. In one sense that proved to be not true: the kingdom was not as near in time as the writers of the New Testament believed. But there is another sense—and an incomparably more important sense—in which the kingdom was near; this is the sense in which it is still "at hand." The event brought the kingdom near and confronted men inescapably with its reality. It was not because they expected the early coming of his kingdom that the first Christians were so passionately convinced of the reality of God's sovereignty; rather it was because they had been made so vividly aware of the sovereignty that they were so confident of the coming. The judgment of God was

123

not a remote future possibility; men stood even then under the awful shadow of it. The mercy of God was not a vague future hope; it was a very present reality which men were even then accepting or rejecting. Nothing less than eternal death and eternal life, hell and heaven, final defeat and final victory depended upon the decisions they were then making.

It has been often pointed out in these pages that beyond the church was the event; so beyond the event is One who is beyond all events and whose kingdom is beyond all human orders and communities. But just as the event is not only remembered but also perpetuated in the community, so the kingdom not only is hoped for but is proleptically present there. Past, present, future— all involved indissolubly in the reality of the church and all caught up in a single act of apprehension when one is admitted to it. The Christian message is urgent and crucial, demanding once for all the ultimate commitment, offering once for all the ultimate opportunity.

It is the historical study of the New Testament which brings to light such meanings as these in the primitive eschatology. Without the historian's help three ways of dealing with the eschatological teaching of the New Testament are open to the preacher or to any other interpreter: he may accept it literally and mechanically; he may reject or (what is the same thing) ignore it; he may interpret it figuratively or allegorically, in terms either of his own poetic or theological ideas or of the dogmas of his group. The third way is subjective and arbitrary; the

124

second way misses the very heart of the New Testament; the first is an impossible tour de force and besides robs New Testament eschatology of vitality and relevance. It is the historian who by setting the teaching within the living context of its own time enables us to see its meaning also for ours and for all the generations.

VII

The preaching of the gospel and the study of the New Testament stand in the most intimate and necessary relation to each other. The very meaning of the preacher's terms—such terms as gospel, redemption, Christ, grace—is the meaning which those terms have in the New Testament. This does not mean that they have meaning *only* there; to say that would be to deny in effect that they have meaning *even* there. But the modern Christian to whom these terms are significant will recognize that their meaning flows from the event to which the New Testament writings are our earliest and most authentic witnesses, and that this meaning can be preserved and quickened only by constant reference back to this primitive deposit. When preaching leaves the New Testament, it ceases to be the preaching of the gospel; or rather, and more accurately, when it leaves the New Testament, it does so because it has already ceased to be the preaching of the gospel. It has lost contact with the distinctive life and thought of the Christian community and with the event in which that community was created, and for that reason finds little

125

value or relevance in the literature produced by that community in the period when the event first occurred. But it is also true that when the study of the New Testament becomes irrelevant to the preaching of the gospel, we can be sure that it has first become irrelevant to the New Testament itself. For whatever else the New Testament is, it arose out of the very heart of the church and in closest connection with the work of its early teachers and preachers. Indeed if any result of the latest study of the New Testament is more assured than any other, it is that the New Testament is by and large the preaching of of the early church. This is perhaps most obviously true of the epistles, but it is just as true—and even more profoundly true—of the gospels.

The preacher and the critic, the preacher of the gospel and the critic of the gospels—they belong together and they need each other! The preacher no less than the scholar is concerned with the gospels; the scholar no less than the preacher is concerned with the gospel. What is most important and most certainly true for the one is such also for the other. For both are devoted to the recovery and interpretation of the event of which the gospels (and indeed the entire New Testament) are the earliest record and the gospel is the continuing proclamation.

Index